First in Line

First in Line

Tracing Our Ape Ancestry

Tom Gundling

Yale University Press *New Haven & London*

Set in Minion type by Keystone Typesetting, Inc.
Printed in the United States of America.

Library of Congress Cataloging-in-Publication Data

Gundling, Tom, 1962–
First in line : tracing our ape ancestry / Tom Gundling.
p. cm.
Includes bibliographical references and index.
ISBN 0-300-10414-6 (cloth : alk. paper)
1. Human beings—Origin. 2. Fossil hominids. 3. Australopithecines.
4. Paleoanthropology. I. Title.
GN281.G86 2005
569.9—dc22

2004059897

A catalogue record for this book is available from the British Library.

The paper in this book meets the guidelines for permanence and durability of the Committee on Production Guidelines for Book Longevity of the Council on Library Resources.

10 9 8 7 6 5 4 3 2 1

For Dr. Frank Spencer, whom I never met
in person but wish I had

Contents

Preface

As a self-conscious species, *Homo sapiens'* consequent introspection sometimes leads to the seemingly logical conclusion that we hold a special, even central place in nature. Even a cursory historical examination of Western thought demonstrates that humans have placed themselves atop the natural world, often justifying this unique position through the belief that we are made in God's image. In contrast, Galileo demonstrated that our planet did not occupy the center of the universe, while Newton and innumerable others showed us that we could understand our surroundings without recourse to supernatural agencies. Darwin taught us that biological evolution is the only logical way of understanding the pattern of biological diversity on Earth. All of these realizations were accompanied by great angst, as they jeopardized *Homo sapiens'* self-appointed position as the pinnacle of earthly creation. This is a book about a relatively recent discovery that perhaps once and for all has knocked the legs out from under the pedestal upon which we have placed ourselves. The discovery in ancient South African limestone caves of very distant human ancestors reified Darwin's hypothesis that we evolved from some apelike form, which firmly reconnected us with the rest of the natural world.

My goal in writing this book is to document in a fresh way a period in anthropological history during which our ideas about what it means to be "human" were severely tested. It is a well-known adage that "fossils do not speak for themselves," and that what is important is the meaning ascribed to them by the scientific community. Anthropology's ability to create meaning for human fossils has always been informed, quite reasonably, by ideas springing from the biological sciences. Specifically, anthropologists' understanding of the evolutionary process is for the most part received from biologists, although how and when new information is diffused from the latter to the former varies.

This study examines the sometimes uneasy relationship between biology (*sensu lato*) and paleoanthropology over the time period roughly between 1925, the year of the Scopes Monkey Trial, and 1950, when a group of eminent scholars gathered on the shores of Long Island Sound in New York to discuss human origins. I argue that during this period a major shift occurred, in which small-brained, bipedal apes from South Africa, once considered mere curiosities, were admitted on to the human family tree. The inclusion of the australopithecines as members of the Hominidae was arguably the last major paradigm shift in the study of human evolution (Kuhn 1970).

Since this is such an essential and formative period in the history of paleoanthropology, it is of special importance to document this shift in thought, and also to investigate possible explanations for why it took so long to occur. Prior studies have emphasized *proximate* causes from within the field of anthropology in attempting to explain the delayed acceptance of the australopithecines as primitive members of the Hominidae (Broom 1950a; Moore 1953; Dart and Craig 1959; Clark 1967; Reader 1981; Reed 1983; Wheelhouse 1983; Tobias 1984; Lewin 1987; Spencer 1990; Landau 1991; Grine 1993; Tattersall 1995). The role of these proximate causes cannot be denied, and many of these influences are borne out in studying the primary literature. This book not only examines these proximate causes as possible explanations, but searches for other, more fundamental answers by looking beyond paleoanthropology to the broader discipline of evolutionary biology.

It is often assumed that obsolete concepts purporting to explain biological diversity were quickly and completely swept away in the wake of the publication of Darwin's theory of evolution by natural selection. In this mistaken view, the scientific community, if not the public at large, underwent a wholesale transformation to a modern view of how the evolutionary process shaped life on Earth. A historical perspective on physical anthropology instead reveals that vestiges of pre-evolutionary approaches to biology and non-Darwinian views of evolution persisted well into the twentieth century. This despite the fact that the australopithecines were discovered many decades after Darwin famously proposed in 1871 that we were the direct descendents of some extinct African ape species.

In the following pages I hope to show that, at least in the case of trying to piece together our own history, the change from a pre-evolutionary to an evolutionary perspective was not rapid and it was not smooth. The acknowledgment that many anthropologists held archaic views of the evolutionary process makes the history more complex, yet it provides a more compelling explanation for the confused reaction to claims of hominid status for the australopithecines. This new wrinkle also helps explain why the eventual acceptance of the South African "man-apes" as hominids was coincidental with the diffusion of modern evolutionary theory into anthropology. Therefore, although ostensibly this book is a historical account and critical examination of the initial South African discoveries of the australopithecines, it is also an analysis of how broader biological issues affected human evolutionary studies, and a reminder that biology continues to influence the field of paleoanthropology.

Acknowledgments

In this book I make use of a very large number of primary sources, and I hope that I have fairly and accurately characterized the ideas of all of the authors. I acknowledge their contributions, for better or worse, to our pursuit of our past.

As this study is a modification and extension of my doctoral dissertation I would also like to thank my Ph.D. committee—Dr. Andrew Hill at Yale, Dr. Dave Daegling at the University of Florida, and the late Dr. Larry Holmes of Yale's Department of the History of Science and Medicine—for all of their help.

I would like to acknowledge the institutions that allowed me access to unpublished resources: the American Museum of Natural History (New York), the National Anthropological Archives (Washington, D.C.), the Library of the Royal College of Surgeons of England (London), and the Bodleian Library of Oxford University. I would also like to thank John Reader for access to his recorded interviews with Raymond Dart, conducted while he was preparing *Missing Links*.

I wholeheartedly thank everyone at Yale University Press for their guidance of a first-time author, especially Jean Thomson Black, who remained encouraging and patient from start to finish. Chris

Erikson did a great job of polishing my sometimes grammatically challenged prose, and Nancy Moore miraculously transformed a virtually bland Word document into something worth looking at. I also greatly appreciate the critical comments I received from three anonymous reviewers; their input undoubtedly made for a superior end product.

Last but certainly not least, I want to thank my wife, Sally, and my colleagues at William Paterson University for putting up with my never-ending whining about how I was never going to finish the book if they kept giving me other things to do!

Prologue

> It is an oft-repeated truism that the knowledge of each succeeding period is built upon the foundations which have been laid in previous ages. The thoughts of to-day are merely the thoughts of yesterday purged of fallacies, and added to by later experience. To understand the position of any science at any particular time, it is therefore necessary in the first instance to take a glance backwards into the recesses of preceding ages.
>
> —D. J. CUNNINGHAM, *Anthropology in the Eighteenth Century*

The August 15, 1959, issue of the prestigious academic journal *Nature* heralded the discovery of a new human ancestor that lived in what is now northern Tanzania sometime during the remote past (Leakey 1959). Christened *Zinjanthropus boisei,* this ancient hominid[1] displayed a unique mix of anatomical features, including traits typical of the living great apes and others associated with modern humans. Newspaper headlines trumpeted the discovery throughout the world, and scholars lined up to heap praise on the scientists who toiled under harsh conditions tracking down our early ancestor. The National Geographic Society rewarded Louis and Mary Leakey with greatly increased funding to expand their research at Olduvai Gorge, with new hominid finds continuing right to the present (Blumenschine et al. 2003). Today, most paleoanthropologists view the *Zinjanthropus* cranium as the fossil find that put eastern Africa on the map and made Leakey a household name.

Shifting our gaze back to 1925, we see in the pages of the same journal an announcement of another fossil discovery in Africa, this one a skull found in a South African limestone quarry near the town of Taung (Dart 1925a). This fossil too was claimed to be a manlike ape representing an early stage in our evolutionary history, and its discovery was likewise reported in the popular press. In stark contrast, however, the scientific community was nearly unanimous in its opinion that the odd-looking ape described by anatomist Raymond Dart had no place on the human family tree.

Since about 1950, paleoanthropologists have accepted small-brained, largely noncultural bipedal apes from Africa as primitive hominids. So why didn't scientists rally around Dart's "Taung baby" in 1925? After all, most scholars at that point agreed that our earliest ancestors had been very apelike. Darwin even went so far as to suggest that this apelike ancestor might have lived in Africa, since this is where our closest living relatives were to be found: "In each great region of the world the living mammals are closely related to the extinct species of the same region. It is therefore probable that Africa was formerly inhabited by extinct apes closely allied to the gorilla and chimpanzee; and as these two species are now man's nearest allies, it is somewhat more probable that our early progenitors lived on the African continent than elsewhere."[2]

Darwin did caution, however, that although this suggestion was based on a simple and logical principle that held for other species, given the scant hominoid fossil record such a suggestion was not much beyond the realm of educated guesswork: "But it is useless to speculate on this subject; for two or three anthropomorphous apes, one the Dryopithecus of Lartet, nearly as large as a man, and closely allied to Hylobates, existed in Europe during the Miocene age; and since so remote a period the Earth has certainly undergone many great revolutions, and there has been ample time for migration on the largest scale."[3]

As I stated in the preface, it is widely believed that by simply looking at the particulars of the Taung discovery one can glean a number of clear reasons for the rejection of Dart's claim that his fossil was that of an early hominid. It is also assumed that later discoveries of more complete remains revealed the true significance of the australopithecines. Here I argue that a more complete answer requires a broader vantage. We must look beyond the field of paleoanthropology, to examine developments within the natural sciences as a whole.

In this book I hope to convince the reader that significant changes in evolutionary theory that developed during the 1930s and 1940s had as much to do with the acceptance of an African ape ancestry as did the discovery of new fossils. And to help us understand the emergence of these theoretical breakthroughs we must journey further still, to a time when the idea of evolutionary change was completely foreign. In the absence of an evolutionary paradigm, ideas about where human beings fit into the grand scheme of things were already in place. To begin, I briefly summarize pre-evolutionary views of humans as a part of the natural world, focusing on the concept of a Chain of Being, or *Scala Naturae,* as a means of organizing nature in which humans were considered the pinnacle of God's earthly creation.

Chapter 2 examines the scientific changes associated with the late Renaissance and Enlightenment periods in European history, during which a general rejection of a static, supernaturally derived and maintained universe took place. Included is a summary of the first cases in which the idea of a more dynamic universe was extrapolated to the organic realm, the logical result being a nascent evolutionary theory. Initial debates about evolutionary change did not instantaneously demolish old viewpoints, and by simply adding a time component to the existing model, theorists preserved the traditional idea of a special creation. However, the "temporalization" of the linear Chain of Being was incompatible with the subsequent Darwinian model for reconstructing evolutionary history, in which essentially limitless branching events were possible within any lineage. The tension between these two models escalated over the last decades of the nineteenth century and persisted into the twentieth.

Chapter 3 summarizes how naturalists interpreted the first hominoid fossil discoveries during the late nineteenth and early twentieth centuries, using the classification system created by the eighteenth-century botanist Linnaeus. This system, based on living species, held that apes and humans were distinct types, or grades, of creatures, and at least initially the fossil record seemed to support this "natural dichotomy." This grade distinction could be maintained while adhering to the simple phylogenetic model inherent in the temporalized Chain of Being. The non-Darwinian principle of orthogenesis was often used to dismiss apes with certain humanlike traits by invoking parallelism, rather than common ancestry, to explain structural similarities.

The main thrust of this study is to explore the time period between 1925 and 1950, which saw a radical transformation of ideas about not only human evolution, but evolution in general. Chapter 4 documents the 1925 publication of Raymond Dart's paper on the fossil remains he found of an "anthropoid ape" in South Africa, and then traces the initial, largely negative, reaction. A historical analysis of the interpretation of *Australopithecus* brings into glaring relief many of the difficulties addressed in the opening chapters. Chapter 4 also examines the discoveries made by Robert Broom during the middle to late 1930s of adult individuals similar to the Taung fossil and of related, but clearly distinctive, forms. Paleontologist W. K. Gregory and his colleague M. Hellman of the American Museum of Natural History visited South Africa with the express purpose of examining the australopithecine fossils, and wrote a series of papers emphasizing the human nature of the dentition. Gregory also challenged the idea of orthogenesis, instead arguing that anatomical similarity was more likely the result of common ancestry.

Chapter 5 focuses on two distinct events that in retrospect were crucial to the acceptance of our African ape ancestry. The first involves the dissemination into anthropological circles of a neo-Darwinian view of evolution as a process. The second is the collection of many additional australopithecine remains at Sterkfontein, and the discovery of new fossil sites at Makapansgat and Swartkrans following World War II. Fossils collected from these sites included the first complete adult crania and, perhaps more important, intact pelvic remains and also the first material culture attributed to the australopithecines. The year 1950 is chosen as an end point, to coincide with the convening of the Cold Spring Harbor Symposium on Human Evolution. This symposium marked a watershed for human evolutionary studies, in which new fossils and new theories dovetailed into the modern field of paleoanthropology.

The epilogue summarizes the main arguments, and then provides a relatively brief summary of significant events that have shaped our view of early hominid evolution over the last fifty years. Our knowledge of our earliest ancestors has grown by leaps and bounds since Dart first described the Taung child, but some new fossil and genetic evidence suggests a more complex scenario surrounding the initial divergence of the hominid lineage from our common ancestor with the living African apes.

CHAPTER 1

The Great Chain Legacy

Long before Charles Darwin and his intellectual heirs began to seriously consider the biological evolution of modern human beings from some "nonhuman" species, Western thinkers formulated a very different way of understanding the natural world around them. For the greater part of the last two millennia, nature was viewed as an unchanging arrangement of living things, organized in a linear sequence with the simplest, most primitive forms at the bottom and the most complex organisms near the top. This "Chain of Being," also called the *Scala Naturae,* reflected the boundless wisdom of some ultimate creative force, and was considered perfect: "The Chain of Being, in so far as its continuity and completeness were affirmed on the customary grounds, was a perfect example of an absolutely rigid and static scheme of things."[1] Perspectives on nature that developed at least up until the fifteenth century assumed the Chain of Being as a foundation, even if other detailed aspects of natural philosophy differed (Fig. 1.1).

The Chain of Being has manifold definitions and interpretations, philosophical, sociopolitical, religious, and otherwise (Lovejoy 1936, Kuntz and Kuntz 1987), but in terms of the biological sciences it can be described as a device designed to impose simple

Fig. 1.1—The Chain of Being, circa 1512 (Kuntz and Kuntz 1987, p. 72).

order on the complex natural world. This chapter briefly examines the development of this idea, and more particularly focuses on the place occupied by *Homo sapiens* by providing an outline of the different types of organisms, sometimes hypothetical or mythological, believed to reside near humans on the Chain. While this review is certainly not exhaustive, it is included to demonstrate that prior to the emergence of evolutionary thought it was recognized that some animals were clearly more humanlike than others.[2] As will become apparent in subsequent chapters, in order for later naturalists working within an evolutionary paradigm to begin contemplating what a human ancestor might have looked like, especially without a significant fossil record, knowledge of which living species were most similar to humans was crucial.

The Chain of Being in Antiquity

As is the case with so many modern Western ideas, our story begins in the minds of the classical Greeks. According to philosopher Arthur Lovejoy (1936), the idea of a universe that contained all possible things can be traced back to Plato.[3] Lovejoy refers to this idea as the principle of plenitude. Basically, since there were no limits on the mind of the creator, all things had to exist, and were present in their pure form in the otherworldly universe of ideas, or essences. Further, each of these archetypes had a representation in the visible world, which humans could more readily comprehend. This meant that everything that could be created did, in fact, exist. Although the observable world was only a dark and blurry reflection of the perfect other-world, it still had to contain a manifestation of every single one of those ideas, or the system collapsed (that is, it was no longer perfect).[4] Variation between individuals of any given type could be explained by the fact that what humans observed was only an imperfect copy of the archetype.

Not only did everything possible exist, but each type was viewed as passing imperceptibly into its neighbor above and below on the Great Chain. This is Lovejoy's second principle, that of continuity. Plato's student Aristotle clearly accepted these first two principles: "Nature proceeds from the inanimate to the animals by such small steps that, because of the continuity, we fail to see to which side the boundary and the middle between them belongs."[5] One important, and logical, outgrowth of these two principles was the idea that between any two known similar organisms, there could theoretically be some missing link. The idea of a missing link was maintained after the emergence of evolutionary thought, but in a modified form.

Aristotle also introduced Lovejoy's third and final principle, that of gradation. Despite the supposed continuity along the Great Chain it was possible to rank animate creatures as more or less perfect, and place them accordingly. Hence the Great Chain was value laden to the extent that it placed everything nearer to or more distant from the creator. Of all secular beings humans were, naturally, considered the most perfect on Earth.

If the immutable Great Chain provided the theoretical context in which to view nature, what were the details of the region where humans resided? In accordance with the concepts of plenitude, continuity, and gradation, it was assumed that organisms existed which very closely approached the human condition. Above were found supernatural entities (angels and gods, for example), which were beyond the purview of human analysis, and below were various creatures that did not quite achieve the level of humanity. The latter group fell into two broad categories. The first were the mythological, yet theoretically possible, wild races discussed by many authors in antiquity. The other category included the various nonhuman primates that were encountered firsthand or occasionally formed a part of travelers' tales. All of these creatures, despite their similarities to humans, were different in some fundamental way. Exactly how they were perceived as different hinged on the prevailing definition of "human," a definition that continues to be modified even today (Cartmill 1990, Stanford 2001).

Throughout antiquity there were stories of wild races that resided just below true humans on the Great Chain. Various classical Greek writers provided accounts of these creatures; for example Herodotus gave a brief account of fantastic creatures living in Libya: "Here too [western Libya] are the dog-faced creatures, and the creatures without heads, whom the Libyans declare to have their eyes in their breasts; and also the wild men, and wild women, and many other far less fabulous beasts."[6] Alexander the Great's travels to the East during the fourth century B.C. exposed him to Indian lore concerning fabulous creatures such as the ichthyophagi of northern India, who lived at the bottom of the sea and ate nothing but fish (Wittkower 1942).

Centuries later, Pliny the Elder offered descriptions of numerous monstrous races in his *Natural History,* written around 77 A.D. Some of these were drawn from older "firsthand" accounts: "India and regions of Ethiopia are especially full of wonders. . . . On many mountains there are men with dogs' heads who are covered with wild beasts' skins; they bark instead of speaking . . . and further to the east of these are some people without necks and with eyes in their shoulders."[7] Another such race was a tribe of people living along the Niger River called the Blemmyae, who "are reported as being without heads; their mouth and eyes are attached to their chest."[8]

It is not certain to what degree people actually believed in the existence of these creatures, and in fact some did deny their existence.[9] In some cases, they may have been exaggerated descriptions of nonhuman primate species; Pliny's cynocephali may have referred to African baboons whose long snouts resemble those of dogs. In other cases these mythical wild races may have actually represented human populations, or pathological individuals, again exaggerated by those documenting them. Alexander's ichthyophagi may have been based on an encounter with a group of fishing people who didn't cook but only dried their fish before consuming it. Regardless, what remains important is that each of these semihumans fulfilled one of the infinite theoretical spaces along the Chain of Being.

In addition to these fantastic creatures, there survive ancient descriptions of primates—certainly of monkeys, and less certainly of apes.[10] As with the wild races, their anatomical similarities to humans were taken to indicate their relative proximity on the scale of nature. It is certain that ancient civilizations knew about monkeys living in their immediate areas. Ancient Egyptians considered the Hamadryas baboon to be sacred from pre-dynastic times onward. Upon dying, especially important people had their internal organs separately mummified within containers called canopic jars, one of which had the baboon carved into the lid. The mummified remains of baboons have also been recovered, indicating the special treatment they received in contrast to other animals. There is some evidence that ancient Egyptians knew of other monkey species, but these were not regarded with the same reverence as the Hamadryas baboon.

Although monkeys are not indigenous to the regions encompassing ancient Mesopotamia, Palestine, Asia Minor, and Syria, some artistic representations of them have been recovered. Monkeys were presumably brought into the region from Egypt, or perhaps could have come from the East. In India, langurs have been revered throughout Hindu history, and the monkey god Hanuman is often shown with Rama. It is probable that classical explorers and scholars also knew of Asian macaques.

Ancient texts reveal that classical Greek and Roman authors also noted endemic monkeys' similarity to humans and to images of monkeys displayed in a variety of artistic contexts (such as vases and paintings). While their use in religious settings has not been confirmed, the ancient Greeks did provide the first natural history–type reports of monkeys. In the *Voyage of Hanno* (fifth century B.C.), along the west coast of Africa Hanno's group encountered "another island, full of savage people, the greater part of whom were women, whose bodies were hairy, and whom our interpreters called Gorillae."[11] Three of these were killed and their skins were taken back to Carthage. That Hanno actually encountered the animal we call a gorilla today is not very plausible; it is more likely that he stumbled upon a troop of baboons.[12]

As head of the classical Greek school called the Lyceum in Athens, Aristotle, along with others, carried out systematic collection and comparison of a variety of organisms, and erected a rudimentary taxonomic system. He divided primates into three types in *History of Animals:* "Some animals dualize in their nature with man and the quadrupeds, e.g., the ape, the monkey and the baboon. The monkey is an ape with a tail. The baboon is identical in form with the ape, except that it is bigger and stronger and its face is more like a dog's; also it is of a fiercer disposition and its teeth are more doglike and stronger. Apes are hairy on the back, in virtue of their being quadrupeds, and hairy on their fronts, in virtue of being manlike. . . . Its face shows many resemblances to that of man: it has similar nostrils and ears, and teeth, both front and molars, like man's. . . . Besides this, the ape has hands, fingers and nails like a man, except that all these parts tend to be more beastlike. . . . In all animals of this sort the internal parts, when dissected, resemble those of man."[13]

Somewhat later, Pliny, in addition to describing the many wild races, also made passing reference to nonhuman primates: "There are also Satyrs in the mountains of eastern India, in the region of the Catarcludi. These are very fast-moving animals, sometimes running on all fours, sometimes upright like humans."[14]

Also, and here it seems obvious that he is not speaking from first-hand knowledge, Pliny wrote: "The types of apes that are closest to humans in shape are distinguished from one another by their tails. Apes are extraordinarily cunning characters. People say they smear themselves with bird droppings and in imitation of hunters put on nooses, set to catch them, as if they are shoes. Mucianus says that apes with tails have played draughts and can distinguish real nuts from imitations made from wax. They are sad when the moon wanes and worship the new moon with great glee."[15] This overtly anthropomorphic passage underscores the point that in ancient times scholars had already identified several kinds of animals that were more or less humanlike in their appearance and perhaps behavior, even if a rigorous taxonomic classification was wanting.

Galen was a Greek physician who wrote a number of anatomical treatises that remained unsurpassed until the Renaissance. While living in Rome, as physician to the emperor, he wrote *On Anatomical Procedures,* which described detailed procedures for dissection. The unavailability of human cadavers led Galen to dissect other primates as proxies in teaching anatomy to his students. Throughout the text Galen justifies the use of nonhuman primates by explaining that since the skeletons of apes and humans are so similar, it follows that the soft tissue structures that use the skeleton as scaffolding must also be very similar: "As poles to tents and walls to houses, so are bones to living creatures, for other features naturally take form from them and change with them. . . . Now of all living things the ape is likest man in viscera, muscles, arteries, veins, and nerves, as in the form of the bones."[16]

Galen may have used rhesus macaques for many of his dissections, but it is probable that he, like Aristotle, was speaking of the comparatively rare Barbary macaque when he mentioned apes, and distinguished these from the cynocephali or baboons: "Choose those apes likest man, with short jaws and small canines. You will find other parts also resembling man's, for they can walk and run on two feet. Those, on the other hand, like the dog-faced baboons, with long snouts and large canines, far from walking or running on their hind-legs, can hardly stand upright."[17]

The Great Chain of Being in the Middle Ages

Throughout the Middle Ages, accounts of both actual primates and of mythical races persisted, often simply transcribed, and accepted uncritically, from the works of classical authors such as Pliny. Little more empirical evidence was generated concerning the natural history of nonhuman primates, and no convincing evidence supporting the discovery of the anthropoid apes appeared until the fifteenth century.

Despite the lack of new biological knowledge concerning these animals, there was no shortage of images of monkeys in the literature and art of the time. In addition, early Christian authors accepted the Chain of Being as an organizing principle of nature and noted, often with disdain, the similarity of monkeys, and other nonhuman forms, to humans. In *City of God* St. Augustine stated:

> Now among those things which exist in any mode of being, and are distinct from God who made them, living things are ranked above inanimate objects; those which have the power of reproduction, or even the urge towards it, are superior to those who lack that impulse. Among living things, the sentient, the intelligent rank above the insensitive, and animals above trees. Among the sentient, the intelligent take precedence over the unthinking—men over cattle. Among the intelligent, immortal beings are higher than mortals, angels being higher than men. This is the scale to the order of nature.[18] . . .
>
> If these races [Pliny's monstrous races] are included in the definition of "human," that is if they are rational and mortal animals, it must be admitted that they trace their lineage from that same one man the first father of all mankind. The definition is important; for if we did not know that monkeys, long-tailed apes and chimpanzees are not men but animals, those natural historians who plume themselves on their collection of curiosities might pass them off on us as races of men.[19]

While the anatomical similarity to humans remained a matter for discussion, what was of greater interest to St. Augustine, and many subsequent authors, was the psychology of these creatures, and particularly their presumed lack of reason. Additionally, it was suggested that only humans had immortal souls, therefore nonhuman primates were placed in an inferior category.

Later in the Middle Ages, the perception of monkeys and apes changed once again, perhaps as they became more commonly encountered due to the increasing introduction to Europe of exotic objects from the East and the Mediterranean littoral. Two of the more widely known compendia from the late middle ages, those of Gesner (1551) and Aldrovandi (1637), have sections on the Simia, and mainly borrowed from classical accounts and sometimes questionable contemporary accounts.

The Discovery of the Anthropoid Apes

Subsequent to the Middle Ages, as a result of rapidly increased exploration throughout the globe, an unprecedented influx of newly discovered organisms arrived in Europe, including the first reliable and sometimes detailed descriptions of anthropoid apes. Unlike earlier descriptions of nonhuman primates (such as Gesner), newer descriptions were based on firsthand accounts of the animals either in their native habitat or as part of collections brought back to Europe. Dutch explorers returning to Europe from the Far East carried with them the remains of orangutans captured in Borneo and Sumatra. Chimpanzees were transported to England from Angola, which occupied a much larger region than the present nation with that name.

One of the earliest somewhat reliable accounts of the African great apes comes from a compendium of travelers' tales called *Purchas His Pilgrimes,* published in 1624. Andrew Battell, a native of England, spent eighteen years in Angola as a prisoner of the Portuguese, between 1589 and 1607. He described "two kinds of monsters, which are common in these woods, and very dangerous. . . . The greatest of these two monsters is called *Pongo* [*Mpungu*] in their language, and the lesser is called *Engeco*. This *Pongo* is in all proportions like a man; for he is very tall, and hath a man's face, hollow-eyed, with long hair upon his brows. His face and ears are without hair, and his hands also. His body is full of hair, but not very thick, and it is of a dunnish colour. He differeth not from a man but in his legs, for they have no calf."[20] It is not known whether Battell actually saw what was presumably either a chimpanzee or gorilla, or if he, like others before him, was simply relating accounts he had heard elsewhere.

In 1641 Nicolas Tulp, a Dutch physician and anatomist, not only provided the first description of an ape brought to Europe, but more importantly included a drawing of the specimen he studied. He described what was probably a juvenile chimpanzee brought from Angola, although some features in the drawing suggest that it may have been an orangutan. Tulp called the animal *Homo sylvestris,* the Latin equivalent of the Indonesian name orangutan, or "wild man of the woods." In 1658 another Dutch traveler, Jacob Bontius, mentioned an "Ourang Outang" he saw on the island of Java.

The year 1699 marks a real turning point in the history of anthropology and comparative biology. That year English physician and anatomist Edward Tyson published a description of a juvenile chimpanzee which was captured in Angola entitled *Orang-Outang, sive Homo Sylvestris: or, the Anatomy of a Pygmie Compared with that of a Monkey, an Ape, and a Man.* Tyson's report was the first detailed comparative anatomical study of a great ape, complete with beautifully drawn plates and a full historical summary of previous accounts of similar animals. Aside from the accurate anatomical information, this treatise went a long way toward eliminating some of the confusion surrounding the distinction between humans, nonhuman primates, and mythical races. In the subtitle, Tyson made it very clear regarding the so-called wild races, including his pygmy, "that they are all either apes or monkeys, and not men, as formerly pretended."[21]

In addition, Tyson placed his study within the prevailing theory of natural order, the Great Chain of Being: "And it would be the Perfection of Natural History, could it be attained, to enumerate and remark all the different Species, and their Gradual Perfections from one to another. Thus in the Ape and Monkey-kind, Aristotle's Cebus I look upon to be a degree above his Cynocephalus; and his Pithecus or Ape above his Cebus, and our Pygmie a higher degree above any of them, we yet know, and more resembling a Man: But at the same time I take him to be wholly a Brute, tho' in the formation of the Body, and in the Sensitive or Brutal Soul, it may be, more resembling a Man, than any other Animal; so that in this Chain of the Creation, as an intermediate Link between an Ape and a Man, I would place our Pygmie."[22] Tyson probably went too far in overemphasizing the human aspects of his animal in order to substantiate his claim for intermediate status between an ape (in this context actually meaning tailless monkey) and a human (Gould 1983). Nonetheless, he presented an exceptional monograph that set the standard for future comparative anatomical treatises (Montagu 1943).

Increasing numbers of orangutans and chimpanzees would find their way into Europe during the eighteenth century, yet the classification of the anthropoid apes remained equivocal. For one thing, it was believed that only one type of satyr, or Orang, roamed the tropics of Africa and Asia. French naturalist Comte de Buffon had possessed an immature chimpanzee that he called a Jocko (possibly a modification of Battell's engeco), and although he made mention of a larger Pongo, which he had only heard accounts of, he suspected that the latter was really just a larger variant of the former and not necessarily another species. Therefore, he did not really distinguish between the Asian and African large apes, but he did recognize the gibbon as a small ape. The third and final ape he discussed is Aristotle's *pithecus*, which he also calls the pigmy, as it was very similar to humans, but stood about one-fourth the height of an average person. Buffon emphasized that humans and apes were very similar in form, especially the large apes, but was careful to differentiate apes from other nonhuman primates: "What I call an ape is an animal without a tail, whose face is flat, whose teeth, hands, fingers, and nails resemble those of man, and which, like him, walks erect on two feet. This orang-outang, or pongo, is only a brute, but a brute of a kind so singular, that man cannot behold it without contemplating himself, and without being thoroughly convinced that his body is not the most essential part of his nature. If our judgment were limited to figure alone, I acknowledge that the ape might be regarded as a variety of the human species."[23] As much as Buffon made of the close similarity in form of the ape and humans, he was explicit in stating how they were actually very different in some other crucial ways: "In the history of the orang-outang, we shall find, that, if figure alone be regarded, we might consider this animal as the first of the apes, or the most imperfect of men; because, except the intellect, the orang-outang wants nothing that we possess, and, in his body, differs less from man than from the other animals which receive the denomination of apes. Hence, mind, reflection, and language depend not on figure nor the organization of the body. These are endowments peculiar to man."[24]

In terms of the significance Buffon attached to the similar physical appearance of humans and apes, it is first of all clear that he, too, was working within the context of the Great Chain of Being. However, he was concerned not so much with classification of organisms into distinct groups as with recognizing the continuity between different creatures: "But, as nature knows none of our definitions, as she has not classed her productions by bundles or genera, and as her progress is always gradual and marked by minute shades, some intermediate animal should be found between the ape and baboon."[25] Despite his emphasis on continuity, his grade terminology is explicit in the suggestion that the animals he referred to as quadrumanous (four-handed) filled the gap between humans and the rest of the animals. However, in this group he included not only apes and monkeys but also the opossums, among others.

The first person to clearly indicate that the African and Asian "orangs" were two different creatures was Dutch physician Petrus Camper.[26] In the 1770s, he dissected the larynx of an orangutan to find out why it could not speak: "Upon the whole, I had an opportunity of seeing seven Orangs, besides the living one, which was sent to his Highness the Prince of Orange. . . . The country they all came from was Borneo, from which island they are first sent over to Java, and so to Holland by the Cape of Good Hope. . . . The Orang Outangs described by Tulpius and Tyson came from Angola, and had both black hair, and large nails upon the great toes. . . . It seems very probable, that Africa furnishes a peculiar sort of apes which are not the Pithecos of the ancients, though these are not uncommon in Angola. Having dissected the whole organ of voice in the Orang, in apes, and several monkies, I have a right to conclude, that Orangs and apes are not made to modulate the voice like men."[27] Camper, like Buffon, took a functional approach to classification; noting that humans possessed two hands, not four, he erected an ordinal distinction for humans called the Bimana, and Quadrumana for the four-footed mammals, including the apes.

Linnaeus and the *Systema Naturae*

One result of the so-called Age of Exploration was a huge influx of biological specimens into Europe from around the world. It became imperative to erect a system to group organisms in a more rigorous fashion. Swedish botanist Linnaeus took it upon himself to erect just such a system, and is typically credited with being the founder of taxonomic studies. If the Great Chain of Being provided a way of thinking about nature in general, it is in Linnaeus's ambitious works that we find the first detailed classification scheme.

In the *Systema Naturae,* which was to go through a total of thirteen editions, Linnaeus, following English naturalist John Ray, initially placed humans in a group he called the Anthropomorpha. He also included lemurs, monkeys, apes, and sloths in this Order, as he called it, and was therefore the first to make the bold move of grouping humans directly with other animals. However, within this Order, he made no distinction between the various nonhuman anthropoid primates, placing them all within the genus *Simia*, with humans the lone member of the genus *Homo*. The distinguishing feature of the latter was contained within the famous phrase *nosce Te ipsum* (know thyself). As a matter of fact, from a purely anatomical point of view Linnaeus had a difficult time differentiating humans from some of the other animals within the Anthropomorpha:

> Indeed, to speak the truth, as a natural historian according to principles of science, up to the present time I have not been able to discover any character by which man can be distinguished from the ape, for there are somewhere apes who are less hairy than men, erect in position, going just like him on two feet, and recalling the human species by the use they make of their hands and feet, to such an extent, that the less educated travelers have given them out as a kind of man. Speech, indeed, seems to distinguish man from other animals; but after all this is only a sort of power or result, and not a characteristic mark taken from number, figure, proportion, or position; so that it is a matter of the most arduous investigation to describe the exact specific difference of man. But there is something in us, which cannot be seen, whence our knowledge of ourselves depends—that is, *reason,* the most noble thing of all, in which man excels to a most surprising extent all other animals.[28]

Linnaeus, like medieval scholars, fell back on a psychological trait, reason, in order to separate humans from other forms. It must be noted, however, that he had little, if any, contact with nonhuman primates. If he had studied them firsthand, it is likely that he, like Tyson, would have been able to distinguish them from humans based on their anatomy alone.

Later, in the greatly enlarged and often quoted tenth edition of

1758, Linnaeus renamed the Anthropomorpha the Primates. In this edition he removed the sloths but added bats. Interestingly, although mythical semihuman creatures of antiquity and the Middle Ages were by this time discounted by most people, the idea of a wild man persisted in Linnaeus's *Homo troglodytes,* which was added in the tenth edition. As a result of this addition Linnaeus placed his other six varieties of human beings into *Homo sapiens,* to differentiate them from their more hirsute relative. Quite clearly, however, *Homo troglodytes* was referring not to a chimpanzee, but to a hairy human derived from Jacob Bontius's earlier account (Chazen 1995).[29]

While Linnaeus's scheme is in some ways contradictory to the Great Chain concept, since his taxonomy is composed of nested hierarchical groups, and is therefore not linear, he still held a gradistic view of nature *within* his categories. In the first volume of the tenth edition in which he classified all of the known animals, he described six classes, from mammals, at number one, to worms, at number six. This was clearly not a random ordering, and of the eight different orders within the class Mammalia, Primates were ranked as number one. The fact that he coined the name Primates for the group including humans and other structurally similar forms suggests that he thought of this group as the "highest." Finally, within the Primates he delineated four genera, with *Homo* as number one and considered paramount (Fig. 1.2).

That Linnaeus was still thinking in terms of the Great Chain is also shown by his use of language identical to that which had typically accompanied prior discussions of nature: "All living things, plants, animals, and even mankind themselves, form one chain of universal being from the beginning to the end of the world. . . . If one single ring or link is missing in the chain of nature, which is what we must follow to a point, we are immediately diverted from the path into an obscure wilderness; we stumble upon stones, we are hurt with thorns, we stick in the mud, and satyrs laugh and jeer at us as

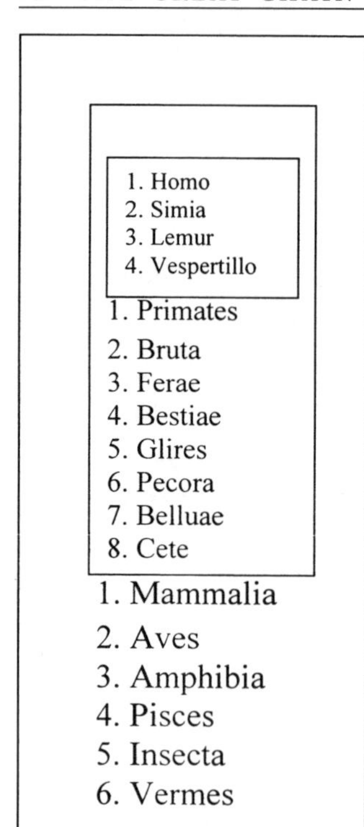

Fig. 1.2—The Linnaean classification scheme (1758). Although this is a nested hierarchy, when it's constructed as shown here an obvious ranking becomes evident.

mere project makers."[30] Here Linnaeus explicates the common belief that the absence of any of the component parts, which are dependent on one another for the survival of the whole, will result in the entire system collapsing.

For a philosopher, the idea of gradation simply meant that all forms, animate and inanimate, could be arranged along a continuum from simple to complex. Where you drew a line between one "type" and another was therefore arbitrary. But for Linnaeus, who was dealing with actual living organisms, a subtle shift in the meaning of gradation occurred. Since he did not have access to all theoretically possible forms, his typological distinctions were *not* arbitrary. Without recourse to the fossil record, he could in most instances easily differentiate one animal "type" from another, and subsequently name and rank them accordingly. It is this modified definition of grade distinctions between organisms on the *Scala Naturae* that became incorporated into the Linnaean classification system. Nowhere was this more apparent than in Linnaeus's creation of a gradistic distinction between humans on the one hand and the members of the *Simia* on the other. Coupled with the notion that nature was fixed, this distinction appeared quite reasonable. The explicit articulation of a "natural dichotomy" between apes and humans would later become a major stumbling block for evolution-minded scholars trying to reconstruct the human family tree (phylogeny) as paleontologists discovered extinct species that displayed traits of more than one extant grade or type.

tion that the planet was very old. Additionally, with the adoption of uniformitarian principles, and the replacement of deluge theory with a glacial theory to explain certain of these strata, "we find no vestige of a beginning, no prospect of an end," as Scottish geologist James Hutton put it.[1] Hutton's view was formalized by British geologist Charles Lyell in *Principles of Geology*, published in three volumes between 1830 and 1833, nearly coincident with the introduction of glacial theory, which was most forcefully espoused by Swiss zoologist and geologist Louis Agassiz. Near-surface sediments formerly attributed to the biblical flood were reinterpreted to be the signature left behind by a series of Pleistocene ice ages. The idea that unsorted and loosely deposited sediments were the result of glacial action, not a cataclysmic flood, meant that the age of the so-called diluvium was not constrained by the biblical timeframe, and was perhaps much older than previously estimated.

It was initially assumed that human history mapped onto the history of the earth, both being the result of a single creation event about six thousand years ago; however, the new geology decoupled the two. Many scientists at the beginning of the nineteenth century accepted a greater antiquity for the earth, although virtually everyone continued to believe that humans had been on the planet for only about six thousand years. But this position also became untenable later in the nineteenth century, when stone artifacts with unequivocal stratigraphic association with extinct animals were recovered in France and England. These discoveries strongly suggested that the human race was older than previously believed.[2]

As early as 1797, John Frere wrote a letter to the Society of Antiquaries in London describing stone tools collected by workmen at Hoxne in Suffolk, England. These artifacts were found in situ, beneath twelve feet of stratified earth in clear association with the jawbone of some large animal that Frere described only as unknown, the implication being that it was perhaps extinct. He concluded, "The situation in which these weapons were found may tempt us to refer them to a very remote period indeed; even beyond that of the present world."[3] The publication of Frere's letter three years later went largely unnoticed, since at the time it was still believed that any objects attributed to humans could be, by definition, no more than a few thousand years old.[4] It was not until the mid-1800s that scientific opinion relented on this matter, when prominent British geologists and archeologists accepted the stratigraphic association of ancient stone tools and extinct mammals recovered by Boucher de Perthes in the Somme Valley of northwestern France (e.g., Prestwich 1860). From this point on, the antiquity of *Homo sapiens* became a serious area of scholarly research.

Upon the realization that humans had coexisted with extinct animals during the deposition of glacial drift, researchers wanted to know specifically when humans first appeared. Although nineteenth-century thinkers were reaching a consensus on an appreciable human prehistory, they attributed the association of stone implements and fossil bones to culturally, but not necessarily biologically, primitive people. In other words, even though the makers of the stone implements were culturally primitive it did not necessarily follow that a different species of human was responsible for creating them.[5] Nonetheless, among those who accepted a great antiquity for humans, some were willing to adopt an evolutionary perspective, and began to try to understand the process and resultant pattern by which humans had evolved from some ancestral primate form.

The Birth of Evolutionary Theory

By the middle of the nineteenth century it was widely believed that the earth was quite old, and it was also becoming increasingly apparent that over the course of time the planet had witnessed considerable geological change. As scholars endeavored to provide scientific explanations for a variety of natural phenomena, the time was ripe for the intellectual leap from accepting the concept of change in the inanimate realm to change in the organic world. The belief that biological diversity could be lost through extinction was becoming commonplace, and discussions proposing an increase in diversity through evolutionary change slowly emerged. The ancient belief in the immutability of species was now challenged in an unprecedented way.

As discussed by Eiseley (1954), the influx of previously unknown organisms into Europe led comparative anatomists and naturalists toward nascent ideas of phylogenetic relationships. Ironically, these same people believed that a greater understanding of biological diversity would illuminate the wisdom of the creator by filling in gaps in the Great Chain. French Enlightenment philosophers and naturalists were the first to seriously propose the idea that organic nature was not immutable (Lovejoy 1936, Greene 1959, Bowler 1989). Modern French philosopher Michel Foucault stated: "Since it had proved possible, by means of experimentation and theory, to analyse the laws of movement or those governing the reflection of light beams, was it not normal to seek by means of experiments, observations, or calculations, the laws that might govern the more complex but adjacent realm of living beings?"[6]

French aristocrat and naturalist Buffon, for example, developed a theory in which preexisting archetypal forms could give rise to a whole series of related species. Although he did not go so far as to discuss the evolution of higher taxonomic groups, he clearly believed that significant biological change could take place over time, largely due to climatic influences.

In England, Erasmus Darwin, a physician by trade, was probably the first person to publish an account of organic evolution in which species and other higher-level taxa arose from a common ancestor. His ideas were first laid out in 1794, in volume one of *Zoonomia,* in which he stated his basic theory that all living things were derived from a single common ancestor:

> From thus meditating on the great similarity of the structure of the warm-blooded animals, and at the same time of the great changes they undergo both before and after their nativity; and by considering in how minute a portion of time many of the changes of animals above described have been produced; would it be too bold to imagine, that in the great length of time, since the earth began to exist, perhaps millions of ages before the commencement of the history of mankind, would it be too bold to imagine, that all warm-blooded animals have arisen from one living filament, which THE GREAT FIRST CAUSE endued with animality, with the power of acquiring new parts, attended with new propensities, directed by irritations, sensations, volitions, and associations; and thus possessing the faculty of continuing to improve by its own inherent activity, and of delivering down those improvements by generation to its posterity, world without end![7]

Dr. Darwin, as he was called, certainly did not adopt the more materialistic position advocated by his grandson Charles, yet he acknowledged that nature was constantly changing, with a progression toward perfection as animals became better adapted to their environment. Like Lamarck (see below), Erasmus Darwin accepted that some internal drive motivated animals toward perfection, and that traits acquired during their lifetime were heritable.

The first "modern" exposition of evolutionary theory is usually attributed to French naturalist Jean Baptiste Lamarck, especially as outlined in his 1809 text, *Zoological Philosophy*.[8] Lamarck had an early interest in botany, but later became an expert in invertebrate zoology, and shelled creatures in particular, at the Museum of Natural History in Paris. Today he is mostly remembered for promoting an erroneous mechanism by which evolution could occur, the so-called inheritance of acquired traits. Like many others of his time, Lamarck thought that biological change was derived from within the organism, as the means by which it strove for higher complexity and perfection. On the other hand, he believed that the external environment in which an animal lived, and to which it was adapted, could only slightly modify the form already in place. He also accepted the theory of spontaneous generation to explain the appearance of at least very simple life forms, which then evolved along a basically predetermined pathway toward higher complexity.

While Lamarck's view of the evolutionary process seems quite foreign now, the scenario he proposed by which humans had evolved from some apelike ancestor was not radically different from what Charles Darwin published almost sixty years later. Lamarck believed that classification should reflect the "actual order of nature," and accepted the taxonomic category of Bimana to distinguish humans from all other animals, placing this family within the order of unguiculate mammals. As for the derivation of humans from some lower form: "As a matter of fact, if some race of quadrumanous animals, especially one of the most perfect of them, were to lose, by force of circumstances or some other cause, the habit of climbing trees and grasping the branches with its feet in the same way as with its hands, in order to hold onto them; and if the individuals of this race were forced for a series of generations to use their feet only for walking, and to give up using their hands like feet; there is no doubt, according to the observations detailed in the preceding chapter, that these quadrumanous animals would at length be transformed into bimanous, and that the thumbs on their feet would cease to be separated from the outer digits, when they only used their feet for walking."[9]

It is noteworthy that Lamarck, and later Charles Darwin, both stated that it was the evolution of bipedal locomotion that served as the first great step in the differentiation of humans from some ape ancestor. This suggestion was not immediately followed up, and it was not until the 1940s that bipedalism was reaffirmed as an early human adaptation, preceding the evolution of material culture and large brains (Gundling 2002).

Like Linnaeus before him, Lamarck accepted a sort of nested hierarchy in nature, but maintained that the overall pattern was one of a graded series: "Meanwhile I shall show that nature, by giving existence in the course of long periods of time to all the animals and plants, has really formed a true scale in each of these kingdoms as regards the increasing complexity of organisation; but that the gradations in this scale, which we are bound to recognise when we deal with objects according to their natural affinities, are only perceptible in the main groups of the general series, and not in the species or even in the genera."[10] Since Lamarck made the distinction between humans and other mammals at the family level, he could argue that even though humans were a part of his order Unguiculata, they were the most complex, most perfect, and therefore highest species within that category despite their ape ancestry.

The Temporalized Great Chain

The intellectual transition from the idea of a static view of the universe to a more dynamic perspective that included organic evolution was not a smooth one. To Buffon, Lamarck, and Erasmus Darwin, among others, change could occur, but the possibilities were very limited. They believed that organisms all strove toward perfection along a more or less predetermined pathway, defined by what Lovejoy called the temporalization of the Great Chain of Being: "The Chain of Being, though not observably complete now, would be seen to be so, or to be tending to become ever more nearly so, if we could know the entire sequence of forms in time, past, present, and future."[11]

The temporalization of the Great Chain of Being was a compromise between the old static paradigm and the new evolutionary theory. Foucault has argued that the evolutionary theory associated

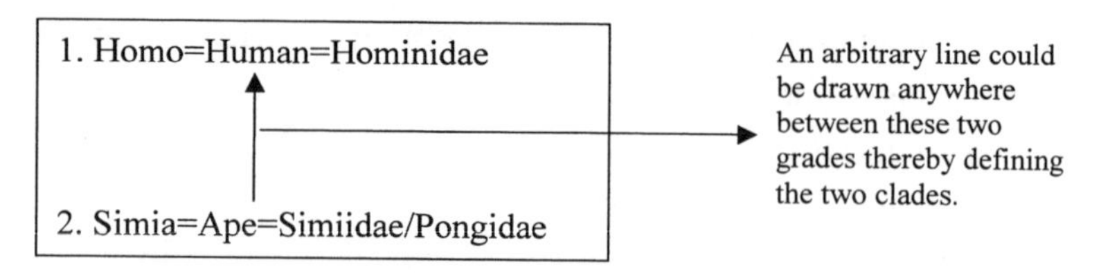

Fig. 2.1—Grade classification could be maintained if phylogeny took the form of a temporalized Chain of Being in which grade terminology was considered synonymous with clade terminology.

with eighteenth-century philosophers and natural historians was fundamentally different from the theory proposed by nineteenth-century naturalists such as Charles Darwin (Bowler 1989). The temporalized Great Chain of Being was viewed as more of an escalator than a fixed arrangement of species, with humans at the top, and change was essentially unidirectional. Thus, the evolutionary process was tightly constrained. This phylogenetic model was completely compatible with the existing Linnaean system of classification. You could maintain the ape/human dichotomy by simply choosing some arbitrary point along the Great Chain at which ape became human. Beneath this point dwelled the apes, scientifically categorized in the family Simiidae (later Pongidae), and above were *Homo sapiens* and their extinct but nonetheless human ancestors, classified in the family Hominidae (Fig. 2.1). At this point, subjective, grade-based classification (such as human vs. ape) was considered synonymous with the more objectively defined evolutionary groupings (such as hominid vs. pongid). Consequently, any species described as predominantly apelike in its morphology was placed in the ape family of primates. Yet according to evolutionary theory there had to have been a time when members of the hominid lineage were more like apes than modern humans. This tension would become acute as the higher primate fossil record grew in the early part of the twentieth century, but would not be resolved in the minds of anthropologists until after World War II.

Extant Cousins

Nineteenth-century scholars assumed that the evolution of *Homo sapiens* had been a foregone conclusion, and inherited the Linnaean grade distinction between humans and apes. Examining the way in which scientists attempted to discover which of the extant primate species was most humanlike reveals these beliefs. In order to begin discussing the evolutionary history of *Homo sapiens*, and the nature of a common ancestral form shared with other extant primates, it became crucial to make this determination. For a variety of reasons it was a question without a straightforward answer. One reason had to do with the introduction of the non-Darwinian concept of orthogenesis. If the temporalized Great Chain led to the notion that the evolutionary process had a predetermined outcome, with humans as the earthly pinnacle, it was almost expected that forms unrelated to *Homo sapiens* could evolve human traits. Similarities between apes and humans were simply due to parallelism (Gundling 2003).

At the same time, however, similarities between humans and primates other than apes were considered possible evidence of common ancestry. Hence some nineteenth-century thinkers argued that you could look at almost any living primate and find some way in which it bore a stronger human resemblance than any other primate. For example, the globular shape of the crania in some New World monkeys was more like a human's than was that of a chimpanzee. The relatively long legs and short arms of humans were like those of a lemur. Based on these observations, Vogt (1864) concluded that it was impossible to determine at what point humans had branched off from the rest of the primate family tree, but suspected that it must have occurred very early in primate evolution. Humans thus had to have an extremely ancient history.[12]

Morse, in his 1884 address to the American Association for the Advancement of Science, presented a similar opinion: "As to his [man's] structural affinities with the higher apes, it has been shown that his relations are not only with these forms but scattered through the whole range from the gorilla down, and osteologically even with the half-apes, the lemuroids, and these in turn have affinities with those perplexing forms, the aye-aye and the tarsier. If these structural affinities are valid, then we must look far beyond and below the present higher apes for the diverging branches of man's ancestry."[13]

St. George Mivart, a devout anti-Darwinian, stated that humans were different in kind, not degree, from other primates, and he, too, argued that they shared no special affinity with any single primate species. Although he acknowledged a widespread belief that humans and gorillas were closely related, he did not agree with it: "There has also arisen a popular belief in the semi-humanity of the Gorilla, or at least an impression that the Gorilla possesses a very special and exceptional affinity to man. This animal is now popularly supposed to be closely connected with that "missing link" which, as is asserted, once bridged over the gulf separating man from the apes. . . . But however near to apes may be the body of man, whatever the kind or number of resemblances between them, it should be always borne in mind that it is to no one kind of ape that man has any special or exclusive affinities—that the resemblances between him and lower forms are shared in not very unequal proportions by different species."[14]

Hence, Mivart suggested that anatomy could not reliably produce a true genealogical tree. He, like others, accepted a certain directionality in evolution, and found it was completely plausible that features seen in humans could appear independently in more than one lineage. If it was not possible to tell which features were the result of parallel evolution from characters inherited from a common ancestor, as Mivart believed was the case, then anatomy was useless in reconstructing phylogenetic relationships.

Despite this confusion in differentiating similarities due to common ancestry (homology) from those attributable to parallelism or convergence (homoplasy), the majority of late-nineteenth-century scholars accepted the apes as our closest living cousins. By 1859 it was quite clear that four distinct anthropoid apes were in existence, two in Asia and two in Africa. Charles Darwin and Lamarck both proposed that of the living primates, it was these "manlike" apes in general and the African great apes in particular that bore the most resemblance to humans. Darwin argued that not only were the apes the closest relatives of humans, but that it was not likely that any other primate form could have given rise to the human species: "The correspondence in general structure, in the minute structure of the tissues, in chemical composition and in constitution, between man and the higher animals, especially the anthropomorphous apes, is extremely close. . . . If the anthropomorphous apes be admitted to form a natural sub-group, then as man agrees with them, not only in all those characters which he possesses in common with the whole Catarhine [*sic*] group, but in other peculiar characters, such as the absence of a tail and of callosities, and in general appearance, we may infer that some ancient member of the anthropomorphous sub-group gave birth to man."[15]

Many others agreed with this position, especially English anatomist Thomas Henry Huxley, a staunch supporter of Darwin to the extent that he earned the nickname "Darwin's Bulldog." In *Man's Place in Nature* (1863), Huxley meticulously detailed the anatomical similarities between the African apes and humans, concluding: "It is quite certain that the Ape which most nearly approaches man, in the totality of its organisation, is either the Chimpanzee or the Gorilla. . . . Thus, whatever system of organs be studied, the comparison of their modifications in the ape series leads to one and the same result—that the structural differences which separate Man from the Gorilla and the Chimpanzee are not so great as those which separate the Gorilla from other lower apes."[16]

Despite such statements, Huxley maintained that humans should be classified in their own family, the Anthropini, and all of the Old World monkeys and apes should be grouped as the Catarrhini. According to Huxley's detailed observations, from a phylogenetic point of view the African apes and humans must have shared a common ancestor and constituted their own natural group (clade) to the exclusion of the other great ape, the orangutan (genus *Pongo*). This inconsistency becomes understandable when viewing the relationships from a gradistic, linear perspective. One could argue for the close relationship of humans and African apes while maintaining a familial distinction. After all, where the line was drawn along a linear continuum to isolate different families was arbitrary. Unfortunately, Huxley did not publish a family tree to show unequivocally his placement of *Homo sapiens* among the great apes.

German scholar Robert Hartmann did not commit to any one of the anthropoid apes being most humanlike; he wrote, however: "On account of their external bodily characteristics, of their anatomical structure, and their highly developed intelligence, anthropoids not only stand first among apes [*sensu lato*], but they take a still higher place, approximating to the human species. . . . [I] accept the Linnaean order of the *Primates,* both for men and apes. I would include men as *Erecti* with anthropoids as *Anthropomorpha* in a subfamily of the *Primarii.*"[17] Hartmann, like Huxley, still placed humans in their own subfamily, separate from the anthropoid apes. If nature was viewed as a slowly revealed divine or at least predetermined plan, then apes would have appeared before humans, but the distinction would have always been clear.

Alfred Russell Wallace, the codiscoverer of natural selection, summarized the state of Darwin's ideas thirty years after *The Origin of Species* in a book simply entitled *Darwinism*. In it he supported the vast majority of Darwin's conclusions, and, based on his own observations and also the work of Huxley, stated that the phylogenetic place of *Homo sapiens* was with the apes: "The evidence we now possess of the exact nature of the resemblance of man to the various species of anthropoid apes, shows us that he has little special affinity for any one rather than another species, while he differs from them all in several important characters in which they agree with each other. The conclusion to be drawn from these facts is, that his points of affinity connect him with the whole group, while his special peculiarities equally separate him from the whole group, and that he must, therefore, have diverged from the common ancestral form before the existing types of anthropoid apes had diverged from each other."[18]

Like Lamarck and Darwin, Wallace suspected that the adoption of bipedality and the freeing up of the hands was the first major change associated with the human lineage: "We must conclude that the essential features of man's structure as compared with that of the apes—his erect posture and free hands—were acquired at a comparatively early period, and were, in fact, the characteristics which gave him his superiority over other mammals, and started him on the line of development which has led to his conquest of the world."[19] Unlike Darwin, however, Wallace suggested that the "probable birthplace of man" was in some part of the "enormous plateaus" of the "great Euro-Asiatic continent."

If the adherence to a temporalized Great Chain model that existed in the minds of scientists was sometimes subtle, expositions in popular publications were not. In 1900, explorer R. L. Garner also supported the proposition that the apes, and the chimpanzee in particular, were the closest cousins of humans: "Beginning with the great apes, which in size, form, and structure so closely resemble man, we descend the scale until it ends in the lemurs, which are almost on the level of rodents. The descent is so gradual that it is difficult to draw a line of demarcation at any point between the two extremes. . . . Next to man the chimpanzee occupies the highest plane in the scale of nature. . . . In the order of nature the gorilla occupies the second place below man."[20] This is a very clear example of how older ideas about nature and humanity's place in it continued. Clearly Garner accepted the Great Chain as an organizing principle and saw the evolution of humans as a final step along a predetermined pathway, with the African apes occupying the rungs immediately below.

Darwin and Natural Selection

Charles Darwin's theory of natural selection as an evolutionary mechanism was qualitatively different from that of his predecessors. At the core of his theory was the idea that evolution was only directional to the extent that populations became better adapted to their local environment. Evolutionary change was thus not predictable in any specific sense, as it relied on the generation of variation that was random with regard to the environment. For Darwin, therefore, the appearance of human beings was not an inevitable outcome, nor was *any* living creature "preordained" for that matter.

More than twenty years after returning from his famous voyage on the HMS *Beagle* (1831–36), Darwin finally published his new ideas in *The Origin of Species* in 1859. This text marked the point at which evolutionary biology matured from a collection of loosely focused ideas to a discipline with a solid theoretical foundation, backed by copious empirical evidence. Darwin amassed an enormous amount of data to support the idea that natural selection was the most potent of evolutionary forces. His position is neatly summarized in the book's closing passage, worth reprinting in its entirety:

> It is interesting to contemplate a tangled bank, clothed with many plants of many kinds, with birds singing on the bushes, with various insects flitting about, and with worms crawling through the damp Earth, and to reflect that these elaborately constructed forms, so different from each other, and dependent on each other in so complex a manner, have all been produced by laws acting around us. These laws, taken in the largest sense, being Growth and Reproduction; Inheritance which is almost implied by reproduction; Variability from the indirect and direct action of the conditions of life, and from use and disuse: a Ratio of Increase so high as to lead to a Struggle for Life, and as a consequence to Natural Selection, entailing Divergence of Character and the Extinction of less-improved forms. Thus, from the war of nature, from famine and death, the most exalted object which we are capable of conceiving, namely, the production of the higher animals, directly follows. There is grandeur in this view of life, with its several powers, having been originally breathed by the Creator into a few forms or into one; and that, whilst this planet has gone cycling on according to the fixed law of gravity, from so simple a beginning endless forms most beautiful and most wonderful have been, and are being evolved.[21]

As is well known, Darwin did not apply his new theory explicitly to humans, stating only that "Light will be thrown on the origin of man and his history,"[22] but in 1871 he published a text that extrapolated the theories introduced in *The Origin* to *Homo sapiens*. *The Descent of Man and Selection in Relation to Sex* was really two books in one. The first half applied natural selection specifically to humans, in part to determine if his theory would work in a way analogous to that which he had previously described for other species. The second half was a discussion of an evolutionary mechanism he called sexual selection, which can be considered a special case of natural selection directed specifically at mate competition and choice.

Darwin's ideas on the course of human evolution were similar in many ways to Lamarck's, even if the mechanism was fundamentally different:

> As soon as some ancient member in the great series of the Primates came to be less arboreal, owing to change in its manner of procuring subsistence, or to some change in the surrounding conditions, its habitual manner of progression would have been modified: and thus it would have been rendered more strictly quadrupedal or bipedal. . . . As the progenitors of man became more and more erect, with their hands and arms more and more modified for prehension and other purposes, with their feet and legs at the same time transformed for firm support and progression, endless other changes of structure would have become necessary. . . . The early male forefathers of man were, as previously stated, probably furnished with great canine teeth; but as they gradually acquired the habit of using stones, clubs, or other weapons, for fighting with their enemies or rivals, they would use their jaws and teeth less and less. In this case, the jaws, together with the teeth, would become reduced in size. . . . As the various mental faculties gradually developed themselves the brain would almost certainly become larger.[23]

Perhaps to eliminate the popular misconception that his theory implied the evolution of humans from one or the other of the existing anthropoid apes (see the Vogt passage above), Darwin was careful to note that his ancestral form was not to be confused with any living species: "But we must not fall into the error of supposing that the early progenitors of the whole Simian stock, including man, was identical with, or even closely resembled, any existing ape or monkey."[24]

Darwin did not include a detailed phylogeny in either *The Origin of Species* or *The Descent of Man;* however, in the former he did include a generalized branching diagram as a visual representation of how natural selection over long periods of time could lead to significant biological diversity. This view of the evolutionary process and its concomitant ramifying pattern was incompatible with the existing paradigm that demanded hard and fast distinctions be made between evolutionary groups along the temporalized Great Chain.

Many of Darwin's contemporaries did not understand the full ramifications of his ideas (Bowler 1989). The Darwinian model meant abandoning the idea that nature could be viewed in a simple linear fashion. The discord between a branching and linear model was commonly circumvented "by lumping together the early members of a radiation with similar, persistently primitive later representatives to form a basal, ancestral 'wastebasket taxon.' "[25] In the particular case of human evolution this meant that many anthropologists still lumped apelike members of the hominid radiation with the living apes, thereby missing their actual phylogenetic significance.

Darwin's view also entailed rejection of terminology such as "higher" and "lower" in describing one organism versus another. What I hope to show in subsequent chapters is that the anthropological community did not begin to truly adopt Darwinian principles until the late 1940s. In fact, I believe that the majority of anthropologists, while enthusiastically accepting the idea of evolutionary change, could not totally overcome the deeply rooted influence of the temporalized Great Chain, in which human evolution was more or less directed, and a simple grade distinction between ape and human could be maintained.

CHAPTER 3

Finding Missing Links

The intellectual chasm between a simple linear Chain of Being and a more complex branching family tree was not easy to negotiate. The temporalized Great Chain of Being had gone some way toward resolving the issue by maintaining the notion of humanity's supreme position in nature yet allowing for evolutionary change. But the compromise of putting the Great Chain in motion did nothing to alleviate the emerging discord between rigid Linnaean taxonomy and the more fluid, relentlessly ramifying phylogeny inherent in Darwinian theory. The Linnaean taxonomic system was erected to organize extant species that were perceived as immutable, which they indeed appeared to be over the course of a human lifetime. Yet evolutionary theory predicted the appearance in the fossil record of intermediate forms that could not easily fit into any preexisting classification scheme.

One way out of this dilemma was to essentially ignore it. As long as fossil species could be placed, even with some discomfort, into the ape or human category, all was well. Moreover, taxonomic placement could then be used to dictate phylogenetic placement. This was possible since it was erroneously assumed that the subjective grade categories of ape and human were synonymous with the theoretically objective evolutionary categories of Simiidae/Pongidae and Hominidae, respectively. In other words, if a fossil form was considered to be a human in a typological, grade sense, then it would be placed on the hominid part of the family tree. Conversely, if a fossil were judged to be apelike overall, it would occupy a branch among the other pongids. With a simple, linear model of evolutionary change as afforded by the temporalized Great Chain, such grade distinctions *could* directly map onto phylogenetic change. If a branching phylogeny was erected then a species would in effect be forced onto one or another branch based on its grade classification.

The Fossil Record

Throughout the nineteenth century, while dinosaurs and other fossil animals were being collected in large numbers (Jaffe 2000), primate fossils remained rare. The first extinct higher primate to be described was a small ape discovered near Sansan in France by Edouard Lartet, a local lawyer with an interest in prehistory (Lartet 1837).[1] Although he did not give a scientific name to the nearly complete mandible in his possession, the species was later attributed to *Pliopithecus antiquus*. Most authorities interpreted the specimen as that of a fossil gibbon (Lydekker 1879, for example). Nearly twenty years later Lartet (1856) described the partial lower jaw and humerus of a larger species, found at the French site of St. Gaudens, that he called *Dryopithecus fontani*. This species was alternately interpreted as a relative of the chimpanzee and gorilla or was thought to be the remains of a very large member of the gibbon family. Notably, it was assumed that any fossil form had to be on a lineage leading to an extant species. This supports the idea that nineteenth-century scientists interpreted the fossil record as revealing a rather straightforward, linear sequence over time, although this was *not* what Darwin had envisioned.[2]

Fossil apes were also recovered in the Siwalik Hills of northern

India[3] beginning in the mid-nineteenth century. Although English paleontologist Hugh Falconer had collected the crown of a canine tooth that he considered to be from a fossil orangutan,[4] a more complete specimen, a fossil palate, was collected in 1878 and placed within the novel genus and species *Palaeopithecus sivalensis* (Lydekker 1879). After a more complete comparative analysis, Lydekker (1896) decided that the specimen could not be generically distinguished from the living chimpanzee, and therefore sunk *Palaeopithecus* into *Troglodytes,*[5] but he maintained the specific distinction based on features that he believed foreshadowed the evolution of humans: "In those respects in which the Siwalik *Troglodytes* differs from the existing African species it shows in a still more marked degree the approach to the human type of dentition presented by the latter, and serves, in small degree, to bind still closer the connection between the *Simiidae* and the *Hominidae*."[6] Although Lydekker's comments regarding the humanlike features of the fossil are of interest, he certainly considered his species to be an ape.

The known ape fossils were important in demonstrating that the Simiidae had been more widespread in the past than at present, but did little to address the question of hominoid phylogeny. *Palaeopithecus*/*Troglodytes* and *Dryopithecus* showed some tantalizing features in their dentition that resembled those of humans, but they were still classified as apes in a gradistic sense.

In addition to the first fossil apes, the first ancient bones attributable to human beings were recovered. Many of the first human fossils were collected from Upper Paleolithic archeological sites in Europe, and were quite clearly the remains of anatomically modern people (such as the famous crania from Cro-Magnon, France, found in 1868). Beyond these Stone Age examples of *Homo sapiens,* other fossils were discovered that despite a strong resemblance to modern humans, were in some ways different. In Europe, several specimens of the now well-known Neandertals were collected during the nineteenth century, beginning in 1829 at Engis Cave in Belgium. A juvenile cranium discovered at Engis with several unassociated adult modern human remains was later recognized as a Neandertal, in 1936.[7]

In 1856 a group of German workers discovered a partial human skeleton in a cave not far from Dusseldorf in the Neander Valley (Neandertal).[8] Noting the unusual nature of the specimens, a local schoolteacher named Fuhlrott notified an anatomy professor at the University of Bonn named Schaaffhausen. Schaaffhausen studied the bones and presented his preliminary findings in 1857. Little interest was generated outside of Germany, but in 1861 an anatomist from the Royal College of Surgeons in London named George Busk translated the paper into English and published it (Schaaffhausen 1861). Darwin's *Origin of Species* had been published only two years earlier, so interest in the Neandertal fossil in England was great. Schaaffhausen interpreted the skeleton as a member of some ancient European race, but did not discuss the possible evolutionary implications: "The human bones and cranium from the Neanderthal exceed all the rest in those peculiarities of conformation which lead to the conclusion of their belonging to a barbarous and savage race."[9]

T. H. Huxley, among others, regarded the fossils as those of a very primitive race, but human nonetheless: "That the Neanderthal skull exhibits the lowest type of human cranium at present known, so far as it presents certain pithecoid characters in a more exaggerated form than any other; but that, inasmuch as a complete series of gradations can be found, among recent human skulls, between it and the best developed forms, there is no ground for separating its possessor specifically, still less generically, from Homo sapiens."[10] Huxley did take note of the simian features of the skull, but found these to be relatively minor in comparison with the overall human appearance of the specimen, particularly regarding brain size. Although Huxley indicated that this was not *the* missing link, it still may have been influential in suggesting that the large brain appeared early in human evolution, possibly prior to the evolution of other key human traits.

Due to their overall human appearance, the Neandertal remains had no more influence than the other so-called primitive races on the reconstruction of hominid phylogeny. Expressing an opinion common for the time, Hartmann (1886) wrote that the Neandertal was the lowest type of human in a continuum from the most perfect to the most primitive: "Although the Neanderthal skull is more like that of the ape than any other human skull with which we are acquainted, yet it is by no means so isolated as it first appears, but is rather the ultimate expression of a series which may be gradually traced back from the highest and most fully developed type of human skulls."[11] This line of thought was completely in keeping with a linear human evolutionary trajectory that was slowly being revealed over the course of geological time. The Neandertal was interpreted as an ancient stage in the progressive refinement of the human species.

Prior to the discovery of the Neandertal remains, a more complete cranium was found on Gibraltar and given a very brief mention in the minutes of the Gibraltar Scientific Society on March 3, 1848. It is unknown exactly when and under what circumstances it was recovered, but it was probably collected by someone mining for lime at a place informally called Forbes Quarry. Sometime after the discovery of the more famous specimen from Germany, the Gibraltar cranium was recognized as being of the same "type," and it was presented as such by George Busk in 1868 to the Royal College of Surgeons and displayed at an exhibition at Bath a year later. Prior to the Bath meeting, Hugh Falconer wrote to a relative: "If you hear any remarks made, you may say from me, that I do not regard this priscan pithecoid man as the 'missing link,' so to speak. It is a case of a very low type of humanity—very low and savage, and of extreme antiquity—but still a man, and not a half way step between man and monkey."[12]

Other Neandertals turned up over the next few decades, including a mandible from La Naulette, Belgium, in 1866 and two fragmentary skeletons from Spy, also in Belgium, in 1886.[13] These latter specimens proved conclusive in demonstrating that the Neandertal specimen was not aberrant, but represented a normal individual from a group of people who once occupied Europe.

Fossil Challenges: *Pithecanthropus*

A simple binary distinction between living humans and apes continued to be made within an evolutionary paradigm as new fossil hominoid discoveries were placed into the ape or human grade and hence the Hominidae or Simiidae clade. The first real challenge to the established ape vs. human view of the world came with the discovery of fossils that displayed key features of both groups. In 1891 fossils collected on the island of Java resuscitated many of the same debates that surrounded the initial discovery of the Neandertals but to an even greater degree, thanks to the truly mosaic nature of the remains.

The Javanese fossils were recovered by a Dutch anatomist, Eugene Dubois, who had traveled with his wife and young daughter to Sumatra in 1887 as part of the East Indies Army, after failing to secure funding through academic means.[14] Apart from his duties as a medical doctor, his primary goal was to collect fossils, in the hopes of recovering the remains of primitive humans. Having been influenced by the writings of German evolutionary biologist Ernst Haeckel, Dubois suspected that the tropics of Southeast Asia might be a likely place to find the elusive missing link. After two very difficult and unsuccessful years on Sumatra, he moved to Java, which he thought might be more promising based on the recent discovery of a human cranium in Wadjak.[15] In August of 1891, Dubois's laborers found the upper third molar of a primate at a site near the town of Trinil, and a month later they collected a skullcap of what he called *Anthropopithecus,* the same genus as the chimpanzee at the time. The following year, he discovered a nearly complete left femur nearby, which he attributed to the same individual. This femur was so modern looking that Dubois eventually changed the name of his creature to *Pithecanthropus,* after the suggestion of Haeckel, and chose the trivial name *erectus* based on the femoral morphology.[16]

Dubois claimed to have at last found the remains of a higher primate species that provided the key link between living humans and the manlike apes. He noted that the Trinil skullcap appeared even more primitive than the Neandertal cranium, particularly with respect to cranial capacity. Whereas the Neandertal had a brain size approximating or even exceeding the modern human average, *Pithecanthropus* was demonstrably smaller. Upon returning to Holland in 1895 after completing his active duty, Dubois traveled throughout Europe lecturing and displaying the actual *Pithecanthropus erectus* fossils: "The native of the Neanderthal has from the very first always been considered as an undoubted, real man. The human character of the *Pithecanthropus* is, however, very questionable."[17]

As with the Neandertals, various opinions emerged in response to Dubois's interpretation. He predictably found support from Haeckel, and also from paleontologist O. C. Marsh at Yale and physical anthropologist L. P. Manouvrier in France, but many of Dubois's colleagues throughout the world were not in agreement. In Germany, prominent anatomist Rudolf Virchow, who had declared the original Neandertal skullcap as pathological, concluded that the remains Dubois had discovered actually belonged to a giant fossil gibbon. In England, Arthur Keith thought it was human, as did fellow anatomist D. J. Cunningham, who stated that "the fossil cra-

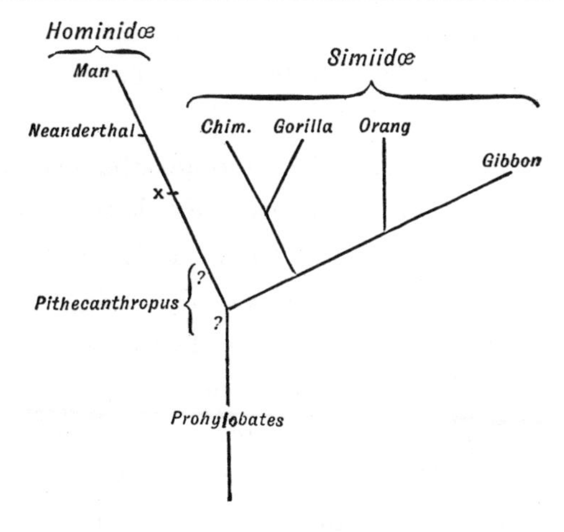

Fig. 3.1—Cunningham phylogeny (Cunningham 1895b, p. 116).

nium described by Dubois is unquestionably to be regarded as human."[18] Again the fossil had to be one or the other, ape or human, and would be given phylogenetic placement accordingly.

An interesting debate between Cunningham and Dubois occurred at a meeting of the Royal Dublin Society on November 20, 1895. This exchange may provide the single best example of the tension between branching phylogeny and Linnaean classification that had developed by the late 1800s. Cunningham presented Dubois with a family tree, and asked him to place *Pithecanthropus* in its proper phylogenetic position (Fig. 3.1).

Dubois was reluctant, but when pressed he inserted *Pithecanthropus* below the point at which apes and humans split. In a letter to *Nature* soon after the meeting he attempted to clarify his position: "In Prof. Cunningham's tree . . . he regards the left branch as all human, the right one as entirely simian and he placed Pithecanthropus midway between recent Man and the point of divarication. Now I could find no place for the fossil Javanese form, which I consider as intermediate between Man and the Anthropoid apes, in any of the branches of *that* tree, only in the third chief line, the main stem, very near to the point of divarication."[19]

Dubois's confusion almost certainly arose because he was thinking gradistically, and was at the mercy of a classification system not geared toward handling transitional forms. He could not place his fossil on Cunningham's tree because in his mind there was no intermediate spot between human and ape, hence the Simiidae and the Hominidae were also distinct. On a linear phylogenetic model he could have easily placed *Pithecanthropus* in between the two extant groups. In fact, he had erected a new family in 1894, the Pithecanthropidae, to emphasize the intermediate nature of his new species. Dubois's solution, like that of later anthropologists, was to focus on the evolutionary pattern using the Linnaean system, and then develop a phylogeny based on this grade classification. Grade and clade were synonymous. His creation of a new family was entirely in keeping with the temporalized Great Chain in that the appearance of the Pithecanthropidae represented an intermediate step along the preordained path toward *Homo sapiens*.

In retrospect, while the discovery of *Pithecanthropus* may have sparked the resumption of debate around the pattern of human evolution, it added little information about more primitive common ancestors with the apes. The vast majority of scholars viewed the species as an archaic kind of human, somewhat more primitive than the Neandertals, to whom it may have been ancestral. The search for the true missing link went on.

Paleoanthropology at the Turn of the Century

During the first quarter of the twentieth century, much of the confusion concerning the evolutionary process in general, and its application to humans in particular, persisted. At the turn of the century

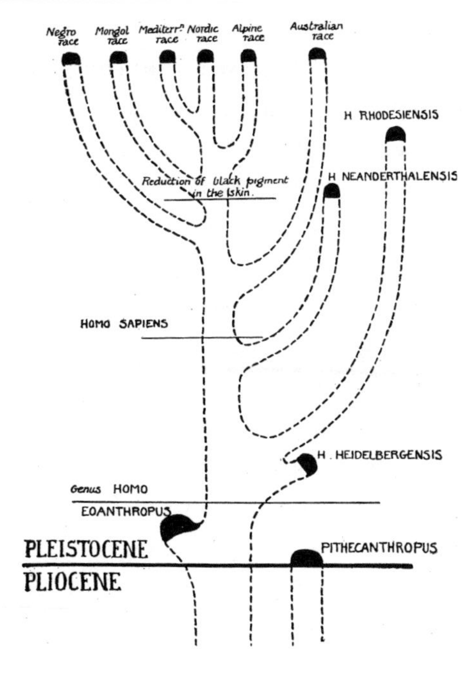

Fig. 3.2—Elliot Smith phylogeny (Smith 1924, p. 2).

most anthropologists still presented unilineal narratives and representations of human evolution, which bore a striking resemblance to what one might expect to find within the context of the temporalized Great Chain of Being (Fig. 3.2).

By the 1920s, many more human fossil remains had been collected in Europe, including a massive human jaw uncovered in 1907 near Heidelberg, toward the bottom of a section of fluvial sediments. The German anatomist who described the specimen, Otto Schoetensack, gave it the name *Homo heidelbergensis*.[20] Additionally, a number of Neandertals were recovered from Krapina, Croatia, between 1899 and 1906. A nearly complete Neandertal skeleton was recovered at La Chapelle-Aux Saints, France, in 1908, and several specimens were found at La Ferrassie, France, in 1909.

Numerous texts on the subject of paleoanthropology began to appear in the first decades of the twentieth century. These were fairly uniform in describing the general pattern of human evolution. It was thought that humans descended from some vaguely defined apelike form, and the earliest known representative of the human lineage was invariably *Pithecanthropus*. In a popular book McCabe (1910) stated that *Pithecanthropus* was the most primitive human type: "Dr. Dubois produced them [the *Pithecanthropus* remains] at the International Zoological Congress at Leyden in 1894, and claimed that he had discovered the 'missing link' in the chain of man's evolution. . . . It may represent some collateral branch of the Primate family, which was extinguished before it reached a human level. Its great interest is that it exhibits a type high above the level of the most advanced ape, a type in which we certainly find the beginning of human characters. In our chief museums (Natural History Museum, Royal College of Surgeons, etc.) the cast of the skull is definitely ranged as early human."[21] The language here is very revealing of McCabe's adherence to the conventional grade structure. *Pithecanthropus* was "above the level" of the most "advanced" ape, and "ranged" as early human in European museums.

Fossil Challenges: Piltdown

The now infamous Piltdown skull, attributed to the novel species *Eoanthropus dawsoni*, was unveiled in London in December 1912 (Dawson and Woodward 1913, Spencer 1990). The remains consisted of several conjoining skull fragments, a partial mandible, an isolated lower canine tooth, and a few stone tools found in association with an extinct fauna. The association of the apelike jaw with the virtually modern human cranium convinced some scientists that encephalization had preceded changes to the dentition. Whether this emphasis on an early increase in cranial capacity was a result of the

Piltdown fossils or whether Piltdown only supported a preexisting view is equivocal. However, the idea that a large brain is what made us human certainly existed prior to the discovery of Piltdown. In fact, many researchers had already suspected that this was the case, probably because most of the fossil humans that had been recovered to date were fairly young, geologically speaking, and had cranial capacities that fell within the range of modern humans. Only *Pithecanthropus* had a relatively small brain case, although some estimates placed it at the very low end of the modern human range.[22] The importance of Piltdown lay in its demonstration that all human traits were not given equal weight in terms of their phylogenetic significance. Since it displayed a large cranial capacity, it was considered human in type regardless of its primitive, apelike jaw, and in fact outside of England the stratigraphic association of the two was very much in doubt. In 1927 Henry Fairfield Osborn, president of the American Museum of Natural History in New York, wrote: "Boule [French paleontologist Marcellin] joined a chorus of American and German opinion that the jaw does not belong with the skull, but is that of a chimpanzee, and that the skull itself in brain capacity is that of a relatively recent type."[23]

In the United States, mammal expert Gerrit Miller of the Smithsonian Institution also questioned the association of the jaw with the skull, and even named a new chimpanzee species based on the mandible, *Pan vetus*. Comparative anatomist and paleontologist William King Gregory of the American Museum of Natural History qualified his discussion of Piltdown, acknowledging that doubts existed about whether the fossils were truly associated. Incredibly, in 1914 he wrote: "It has been suspected by some that geologically they [the Piltdown fossils] are not old at all; that they may even represent a deliberate hoax, a negro or Australian skull and a broken ape-jaw, artificially fossilized and 'planted' in the gravel-bed, to fool the scientists."[24]

Even those who accepted the authenticity of Piltdown, if only for the time being, characterized the species as a fairly recent ancestor (that is, post *Pithecanthropus*) that happened to retain a primitive jaw morphology. Consequently, acknowledging *Eoanthropus dawsoni* as a valid species did not suggest much about the earliest phases of human evolution.

Fossil Challenges: *Sivapithecus*

In the early twentieth century, fossil apes continued to be collected in Western Europe and in the Siwalik Hills of India. Guy Pilgrim, a paleontologist with the India Geological Survey, published a detailed analysis of the fossil apes and monkeys collected up to 1915. Of particular interest was his placement of the species *Sivapithecus indicus* within the Hominidae, while relegating other species to the Simiidae (Pilgrim 1915). *Sivapithecus* was known only from fragmentary remains including teeth and partial jaws, yet Pilgrim thought these were sufficiently humanlike to justify inclusion. The fact that he placed what was clearly an apelike species in the family Hominidae suggests that he was one of the first to overcome the primacy of grade classification in reconstructing phylogeny.

The response to Pilgrim's suggestion is revealing. R. Lydekker, who had preceded Pilgrim in the Siwaliks, commented on Pilgrim's proposal in a short note to *Nature:* "The greatest interest attaches . . . to specimens described as *Sivapithecus indicus,* and referred to the family Hominidae. . . . The author concludes his article with observations on the evolution of the Anthropoidea, in the course of which it is suggested that Sivapithecus should take its place as a side-branch from the main stem which gave rise to man himself. . . . While the article is full of interest, further consideration is advisable before the author's views are accepted in their entirety."[25] Again the language is telling; the branch that gave rise to humans is the *main* branch.

William King Gregory, an expert on mammalian dentition, also responded, with a short note in the journal *Science:* "The reviewer regrets to report that after a careful study of the evidence he believes Dr. Pilgrim has erred in attributing the above mentioned human characteristics to *Sivapithecus*. . . . The reviewer would also dissent from Dr. Pilgrim's allocation of *Sivapithecus* to the Hominidae, preferring to place it by definition in the Simiidae, since it had ape-like canines and front premolars, and, as the reviewer interprets the evidence, also an ape-like symphysis."[26] Gregory's comment that the apelike features of *Sivapithecus* must *by definition* result in classification among the Simiidae is very instructive. It did not seem to matter to Gregory if *Sivapithecus* was related to humans in a phylogenetic sense. The features of the dentition allied the species with other apes regardless of any "human" features.

The following year, in a much longer monograph, he added: "However, even if it should be thoroughly established that Sivapithecus is directly ancestral to the Hominidae, this would not, in the reviewer's opinion, warrant its removal from the Simiidae to the Hominidae, unless it could be shown that in the totality of its skeletal characters the genus was more manlike than ape-like."[27] What is fairly explicit here is the continued tension between phylogenetic statements and classification. If Gregory accepted that the Hominidae should include *all* of the species within the evolutionary lineage once separate from the great ape lineage, his position would require a period during which the earliest members of the human lineage would *not* be more manlike than apelike "in the totality" of their "skeletal characters." Yet despite *Sivapithecus*'s possible placement on that lineage, Gregory chose to place this species in the Simiidae, indicating that grade-based taxonomy held priority over phylogenetic considerations. This is particularly noteworthy as Gregory was perhaps the most outspoken advocate of a great ape ancestry for modern humans.

Another reviewer of Pilgrim's proposal was anatomist Grafton

Elliot Smith, who believed that "the brain led the way" in human evolution. In keeping with this hypothesis he concluded that unless there were human features of the brain, it did not matter what the teeth looked like: "Even if the resemblances of the teeth of *Sivapithecus* to those of Man were closer than they are, this would not justify the inclusion of the former in the Human Family. It would merely suggest its kinship to the ancestors of the Family."[28]

English anatomist Arthur Keith also disagreed with Pilgrim. In a manuscript written in 1915 he stated that there was no reason to place *Sivapithecus* outside of the Simiidae: "I am of opinion, from the characters described by Dr. Pilgrim, that Sivapithecus is a robust anthropoid belonging to the genus Dryopithecus or to a genus nearly allied to Dryopithecus. . . . It will be thus seen that on the evidence at present available, the proper place for Sivapithecus . . . is not in the human but in the anthropoid phylum."[29]

In sum, fossils discovered during the nineteenth and early twentieth centuries reified the Linnaean dichotomy between apes and humans. Theoretical rhetoric hypothesizing apelike ancestors notwithstanding, primitive features of human fossils and derived traits discovered in otherwise apelike skulls were duly noted, but the grade distinction was maintained. Family trees constructed based on this binary system were either simple and unilineal or showed clearly separate branches for apes and humans.

Part of the reason this false dichotomy could be maintained was because the gradistic categories of ape and human were not clearly defined. It seems as though some humanlike qualities were more important than others. Despite its primitive dentition, the humanlike cranium of Piltdown led everyone to accept it as a human ancestor. Similarly, despite the relatively small cranial capacity of *Pithecanthropus* it was still much larger than that of any ape, and the femur was clearly human. The hominid status of *Sivapithecus,* on the other hand, was argued based on dental features. These were not considered sufficient for categorizing the species as a human. The reason for this probably involved the supposed evolutionary force called orthogenesis, which was widely accepted at the time and maintained that evolution occurred in a directed fashion. Within the theoretical context of a temporalized Great Chain humans were the ultimate goal of the evolutionary process, maintaining their place atop the natural world. Orthogenesis predicted that independent lineages in the past would have striven toward the same end (that is, *Homo sapiens*); therefore fossils exhibiting some "human-like" traits could be interpreted as mere parallelisms and dismissed as failed evolutionary experiments. As we shall see in the next chapter, the scholarly debate involving the *Sivapithecus* remains was repeated with the discovery in 1924 of an enigmatic skull of a juvenile higher primate in a remote South African limestone quarry.

CHAPTER 4

The Southern Ape

During the first decades of the twentieth century, the Linnaean taxonomic system, in which apes and humans were considered distinct kinds of higher primates, continued to function in an evolutionary context as long as fossils supported this "natural" dichotomy. The fossil record seemed to corroborate the Linnaean dichotomy, revealing two groups of extinct forms: those that had crossed some poorly defined human threshold and were therefore members of the Hominidae, and some which had not and were grouped among the Pongidae: "Darwin and Huxley proceeded of course from comparative anatomy; practically speaking, human or anthropoid fossils were unknown. Their allying of man and the apes was a great victory for the day. At the same time, however, men were men and apes were apes."[1] In an attempt to accommodate both this simple grade dichotomy and the idea of evolutionary change, scholars reverted to the Great Chain of Being in its temporalized form. Family trees published during this time period reflect the idea of an inexorable ascension toward *Homo sapiens,* with numerous side branches representing failed evolutionary attempts at becoming human.

Fossil Challenges: *Australopithecus*

In 1925 paleoanthropology was still a relatively new discipline with very few full-time practitioners, most of whom were trained in other areas, most often anatomy (Spencer 1981). The story of human evolution was interpreted as being fairly straightforward. Humans had evolved from some as yet unknown apelike ancestor, perhaps similar to *Dryopithecus* or *Sivapithecus,* and passed through a variety of primitive stages represented by *Pithecanthropus, Eoanthropus,* and the Neandertals before evolving into their modern form.[2] Debate surrounding the latter taxa had to do with their phylogenetic position relative to modern human ancestry, *not* their status as human or nonhuman. It is within this context that *Australopithecus africanus* was introduced by Raymond Dart to the scientific establishment. In retrospect, the discovery of *Australopithecus* in 1924 signaled the beginning of a paradigm shift in human evolutionary studies (Gundling 1999). Although it took nearly twenty-five years for this change to take hold, it could be argued that the acceptance of small-brained "bipedal apes" from Africa as direct human ancestors marked the final fundamental change in thought regarding the transformation of ape into human.

Raymond Arthur Dart was born and raised in Australia, and went on to receive his medical degree from Sydney University. He later went to England, working under the tutelage of neuroanatomist Grafton Elliot Smith, and during this period spent one year in the United States, studying at Washington University in St. Louis. In 1923 Elliot Smith, among others including Arthur Keith, encouraged Dart to take a newly opened position as chair of anatomy at the nascent University of the Witwatersrand Medical School in South Africa. Dart reluctantly accepted, not wanting to leave the stimulating intellectual environment he had found in London, and left for Johannesburg with his wife, Marjorie.[3] Soon after arriving in South

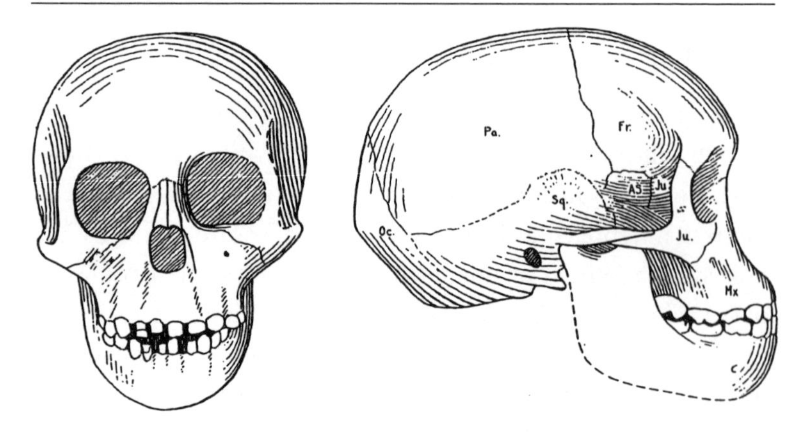

Fig. 4.1—Type specimen of *Australopithecus africanus* Dart discovered at Taung, South Africa, in 1924 (Broom 1925b, p. 413).

Africa, in an effort to build the university's anatomical collections, Dart began encouraging his students to bring him specimens. One of his students presented him with a fossil baboon skull that had been recovered at a local lime quarry. Intrigued, he asked the Northern Lime Company foreman to set aside further fossils should they present themselves. In November of 1924, a colleague of Dart's, a geologist from the University of Witwatersrand named R. B. Young, presented Dart with two crates full of fossil bones he had transported from the Buxton quarry near the town of Taung.[4] To Dart's delight, one of these crates contained the fossilized skull of a young anthropoid ape (Fig. 4.1). The face and lower jaw were intact, along with a full set of milk teeth and the first adult molars. The bones of the brain case were destroyed, but a natural brain cast, or endocast, was preserved. Dart's training in neuroanatomy drew his attention to the latter, which seemed to exhibit humanlike features despite its small size. Realizing that he had something of possibly great importance, he set about the tedious task of removing the sediments adhering to the fossil, and began preparing a short manuscript for publication.

On February 7, 1925, Dart's five-page paper appeared in the journal *Nature*, describing the fossil remains of the young primate (Appendix A.1).[5] He emphasized the many traits that distinguished the fossil from living and extinct apes, and that seemed to be more human in their appearance: "[The fossil ape] represents a fossil group distinctly advanced beyond living anthropoids in those two dominantly human characters of facial and dental recession on the one hand, and improved quality of the brain on the other."[6]

Dart not only placed the fossil in a new genus and species, *Australopithecus africanus,* but he also erected a new primate family for his specimen, the Homosimiadae. Like Dubois thirty years earlier, Dart was thinking gradistically, and wrote that *Australopithecus* "exhibits an extinct race of apes intermediate between living anthropoids and man."[7] From an evolutionary point of view it is not possible to have a fossil form intermediate between two living species. On the other hand, thinking along gradistic lines, with the evolutionary path proceeding along the temporalized Great Chain of Being, this statement makes sense. *Australopithecus* was "advanced" beyond the living ape grade, so it was not classified in the Pongidae, but on the other hand Dart still referred to it as an anthropoid, so it could not be placed within the Hominidae. He had no choice but to erect a new family.[8]

In his family tree, published several months later (Fig. 4.2), Dart described *Australopithecus* as typifying the ancestral stock from which all later Hominidae arose. This figure is similar to other phylogenies that used a tree metaphor. There was a central trunk, representing the main path of evolutionary change, and various branches showing species that had diverged from this path. The tension between phylogeny and taxonomy is evident in that Dart viewed *Australopithecus* as a possible human ancestor, yet classified it as an ape. By virtue of this clarification, others suggested, just as Gregory had done with *Sivapithecus* a decade earlier, the Taung fossil could not, by definition, be placed directly on the human lineage.

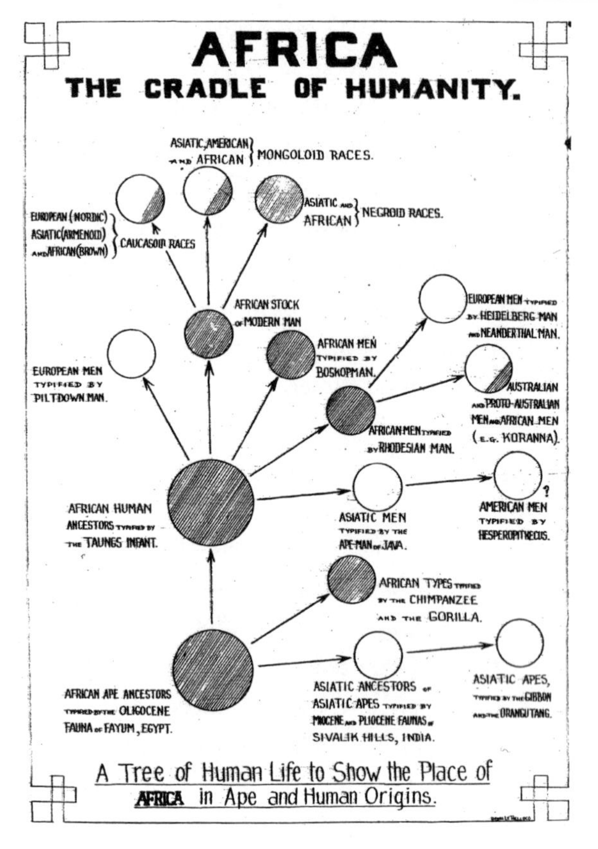

Fig. 4.2—Dart phylogeny (Dart 1925b, p. 1154).

The Response

The response by the scientific community was rapid and nearly unanimous: while Dart had discovered an interesting fossil ape, it had nothing to do with human evolution (Appendix A.2). The first reaction came from four prominent British scientists just one week following Dart's paper, also in *Nature*. The most favorable review came from Dart's former mentor, Grafton Elliot Smith, who, while noting that the fossil was "an unmistakable anthropoid ape that seems to be much on the same grade of development as the gorilla and the chimpanzee," was nonetheless impressed by the endocranial evidence.[9] In particular he was impressed by the relative position of two grooves, or sulci, visible in the cast: "The most suggestive feature is the position of the sulcus lunatus and the extent of the parietal expansion that has pushed asunder the lunate and parallel sulci—a very human feature."[10] For years Elliot Smith had championed the idea that brain expansion had preceded other important changes in human evolution. According to him and others, this was the initial change that allowed for the subsequent evolution of the constellation of behaviors unique to modern humans. He was quick to caution, however, that with only a single specimen that was of unknown geological age—and, in fact, not even fully prepared—it was impossible to make a final judgment as to the proper phylogenetic placement of the fossil.

In an article published simultaneously in a popular periodical, Elliot Smith accepted Dart's observation that the brain cast of *Australopithecus* showed some human features—particularly in the expansion of the parietal area, which suggested greater intelligence than that of any living ape—but again emphasized caution: "The fact that the brain had not attained proportions clearly differentiating it from that of the gorilla or chimpanzee emphasises the need for caution in claiming the nearer kinship of *Australopithecus* to the human family."[11] Like Dart, Elliot Smith noted certain humanlike features of the new species, yet due to the grade distinction he made, he thought it most judicious to place the fossil among the other apes until further evidence proved otherwise. This conclusion made it very difficult to think of Taung as a human ancestor.

The harshest criticism came from Arthur Smith Woodward of the Natural History Museum of London. Woodward had written extensively on the large-brained Piltdown remains, and more recently on the Broken Hill fossil from Rhodesia,[12] which also possessed a large cranium, so it is not surprising that he was so dismissive of Dart's claims (Dawson and Woodward 1913, Woodward 1921). He insisted that the fossil's supposed humanlike features, such as small canine teeth and the lack of a bony ridge on the lower jaw called a simian shelf, could be found in immature chimpanzees and adult members of the fossil ape *Dryopithecus,* the remains of which Woodward had described a decade earlier (Woodward 1914). The suggestion that the immaturity of the fossil precluded any definitive statements about its relationship with other forms was a point that Elliot Smith had also made. Furthermore, in what can only be read as a complete dismissal of Dart's main point regarding the phylogenetic position of the fossil, Woodward stated: "In the absence of knowledge of the skulls of the fossil anthropoid apes represented by teeth and fragmentary jaws in the Tertiary formations of India, it is premature to express any opinion as to whether the direct ancestors of man are to be sought in Asia or in Africa. The new fossil from South Africa certainly has little bearing on the question."[13]

Anatomist W. L. H. Duckworth also noted that due to the young age of the Taung baby, "the elimination and detachment of features influenced largely by the factor of age demand special attention." Still, he wrote that some of the characters enumerated by Dart, particularly those of the brain endocast and several facial features, "appear to me to possess a higher value in evidence than others." Duckworth did not appear to be swayed one way or another, and like Elliot Smith, chose to reserve judgment until a more complete analysis was undertaken, or more complete adult individuals were recovered.

The fourth reviewer, and arguably the most influential student of human evolution at the time, Arthur Keith, apparently saw nothing extraordinary in the Taung find, as indicated by the brief mention he gave the fossil in a journal entry from January 1925: "Had article from Dart describing a new 'missing link.' I advised publication and got a reprint on Tuesday morning. Worked it over and saw it was anthropoid. Wrote to Dart."[14] In his *Nature* comments he commended Dart on his discovery, yet concluded: "On the evidence now produced one is inclined to place *Australopithecus* in the same group or subfamily as the chimpanzee and gorilla. It is an allied genus. It seems to be near akin to both, differing from them in shape of the head and brain and in a tendency to the retention of infantile characters."[15] Keith agreed with Dart's assertion that there were some unusual features in the Taung fossil, but did not feel that these were sufficient to justify Dart's linking of the fossil with later human evolution. Clearly what differed was Keith's interpretation of the humanlike traits, not his opinion about whether or not they existed. Any human qualities, including the tiny supraorbital ridges, the small size of the canine teeth, and the almost complete lack of a space between adjacent anterior teeth (diastema), he dismissed as simple parallelisms. This was an easily defensible assertion given the widespread acceptance of orthogenesis as a potent evolutionary force.

For Dart, the essential human qualities were to be found in the head, although he did bring up the issue of bipedalism, an important feature since it would allow the hands to be employed for uses other than locomotion. Since no postcranial fossils were recovered with the skull, Dart relied on estimating the position of the head on the body, which differs between bipeds and quadrupeds: "That hominid characters were not restricted to the face in this extinct primate group is borne out by the relatively forward situation of the foramen magnum. . . . It is significant that this [cranial] index . . . points to the assumption by this fossil group of an attitude appreciably more erect than that of modern anthropoids."[16] Keith also took issue with Dart's claim of erect posture: "We cannot be certain of posture until we find a bone of the lower limb. One cannot see any character in the skull which justifies the supposition of an erect posture."[17]

Keith had written Dart congratulating him on the discovery, and Dart reciprocated on February 26, thanking Keith but also responding to the criticism in *Nature:* "But if any errors have been made, they are all on the conservative (ape) side and it is certain that subsequent work will serve only to emphasise the *human* characters. Broom [paleontologist Robert] was here last week-end and we went over it very carefully together. He places it in the direct line and if anything nearer to Piltdown man than I have cared to place it. . . . the premaxilla-maxillary suture is humanoid and not anthropoid. Further the first permanent molars, although large (14mm × 14mm), are remarkably human in their characters—cusps etc. . . . There seems therefore very little doubt that my Homo-simiadae is a justifiable group and this Broom fully concurs in. The brain size and character along with these added points carry us right out of the living anthropoid series."[18]

Further reaction came at a meeting of the Royal Physical Society of Edinburgh on March 16, from Professor Arthur Robinson. He compared Dart's figures of the Taung primate with similar figures made of four chimpanzees from the Edinburgh University anatomy museum, and concluded that "the Taungs[19] specimen was the distorted skull of a chimpanzee just over four year old, probably a female" (Anon. 1925). Clearly the British establishment was at best reserved and at worst dismissive of Dart's suggestion that *Australopithecus* represented an early human ancestor.

All of the initial reviewers based their conclusions on the brief text, tiny photographs, and figures contained in Dart's *Nature* and *Illustrated London News* articles. However, in June, a cast of the Taung fossil was put on display in London as part of the South African Pavilion of the British Empire Exhibition at Wembley (Dart 1925b). On June 9, Elliot Smith "exhibited, and made remarks upon" the cast (Smith 1925c). In May, when the cast first arrived, Elliot Smith had given a lecture at University College in which he stated:

"Prof. Raymond Dart's discovery at Taungs, in Bechuanaland, of a fossil anthropoid skull had been claimed as the link that hitherto had been missing. But it was certainly not one of the really significant links for which they were searching. It was an unmistakable ape, nearly akin to those still living in Africa, the chimpanzee and the gorilla, and there was no justification for the creation of a new family, though it certainly represented a new genus. . . . In spite of the fact that many of his arguments were untenable, some of his general conclusions were confirmed."[20]

Keith went to see the fossil cast, and noted in his diary that he "spoke on Taungs skull that cost me a visit to Wembley."[21] He was apparently not impressed, and on June 22 wrote a letter to *Nature* complaining that those who wished to view the fossils "must go to Wembley and peer at them in a glass case." His opinion had not changed, and he again concluded that "in every essential respect the Taungs skull is that of a young anthropoid ape."[22]

Dart, however, was not without his supporters. Scottish physician and paleontologist Robert Broom had spent a significant portion of his life in South Africa, collecting and describing mammal-like reptiles from the Karroo region. Although Broom's role in the history of *Australopithecus* becomes more prominent beginning in 1936, he was one of the few people who actually studied the original fossil in 1925, and was the only one who completely supported Dart from the beginning: "in this new form discovered by Prof. Dart we have a connecting link between the higher apes and one of the lowest human types."[23] Although Broom was supporting Dart's contention of human ancestry for the Taung baby, his language belies adherence to the temporalized chain model of phylogeny. *Australopithecus* occupied that fuzzy space where ape and human were not quite distinct.

While Broom agreed with Dart concerning the morphology of the Taung child, he believed that the skull was, geologically speaking, very young. This claim was based on a handful of associated faunal remains that did not appear to Broom to be very different from related extant species: "I think it can be safely asserted that the Taungs skull is thus not likely to be geologically of great antiquity—probably not older than Pleistocene, and perhaps even as recent as the *Homo rhodesiensis* skull."[24] This turned out to be important, since some of Dart's detractors, notably Keith, used the young geologic age to argue against the possibility of Taung being a human ancestor: "Students of man's evolution have sufficient evidence to justify them in supposing that the phylum of man had separated from that of the anthropoid apes early in the Miocene period. The Taungs ape is much too late in the scale of time to have any place in man's ancestry."[25] The perceived young age of the fossil, and of other related fossils later discovered by Broom, would present a major challenge to claims for their role as direct human ancestors for decades.

Later that year, Broom wrote a longer article for *Natural History,* a popular periodical published by the American Museum of Natural History in New York. He continued to champion Dart's contention that the species from Taung represented an intermediate form: "The study of the teeth renders it pretty certain that *Australopithecus* stands somewhere between the chimpanzee and man. . . . It will be seen from what has been said that *Australopithecus* forms a most satisfactory connecting link between the anthropoid apes below and the various human and sub-human types above."[26] The gradistic view here is obvious, and it is also evident in the phylogeny accompanying both this essay and Broom's previous *Nature* article (Fig. 4.3). That this is a pictorial representation of the Chain of Being, and not a phylogeny in the modern sense, is apparent in that humans stand alone atop the figure, and other extant forms are placed *below* extinct human ancestors. This is an excellent example of the way in which it was possible to state that *Australopithecus* was a human ancestor while maintaining that it was still an ape.

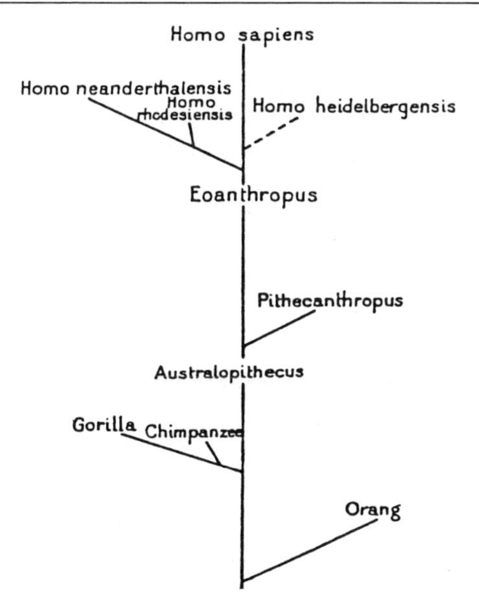

Fig. 4.3.—Broom phylogeny (Broom 1925a, p. 571).

William J. Sollas, a former student of T. H. Huxley's and a geologist at Oxford from 1897 until his death, was also initially skeptical of the Taung fossil's human affinities. In March of 1925 he wrote to Broom, with whom he was a regular correspondent: "My conclusions based on the absurdly minute illustrations accompanying Dart's communication in *Nature* was that the skull represents simply a new species of chimpanzee or gorilla."[27] Subsequently, per Sollas's request, Broom sent him drawings of sagittal sections of the Taung cranium to compare with living apes and humans. His analysis demonstrated fairly conclusively that the South African anthropoid was not a chimpanzee or gorilla, and that the ways in which it differed were somewhat human. However, he stopped short of saying exactly what the likeness meant in a phylogenetic sense: "It is abundantly clear that in a number of significant morphological characters, such as complete absence of the frontal torus, position of the nasion, greater magnitude of the parietal arc, reduced prognathism and shortening of the maxillary region, Australopithecus makes a nearer approach to the Hominidae than any existing anthropoid ape."[28] He was a bit more forthcoming in another letter to Broom in May: "It is true we haven't a very large collection of young chimpanzee skulls in our collection, but quite enough, I think, to go on with, and the more I compare them with Taungs the more difference I see, and the more human Taung appears. . . . The forehead is as thoroughly human as it is not anthropoid. It gives one a lot to think about."[29]

Sollas was very critical of Keith's assertions regarding *Australopithecus*. In a letter to Broom in May he accused Keith of influencing what did and did not get published in *Nature*, and in another letter in July he wrote to Broom: "You will probably have read his [Keith's] communication to 'Nature' by the time you read this. . . . I am truly astonished. He makes the rashest statements in the face of evidence. Never quotes an author but to misrepresent him, generalises on single observations, and indeed there is scarcely a single crime in which he is not adept."[30]

Aside from Broom and Sollas, Dart found little support from his colleagues. In April, Eugene Dubois wrote to Keith to clarify a few points surrounding the account of the discovery of *Pithecanthropus* contained in Keith's new edition of *The Antiquity of Man* (Keith 1925a). At the end of the letter Dubois added: "I have also to thank you for the sending of the reprint from 'Nature' on Australopithecus. I quite agree with your and Elliot-Smith's opinion (and so does Bolk), that Dart has found an interesting (especially from a distributional point of view) anthropoid ape, at least nearly akin with the gorilla."[31]

In the United States during the 1920s there were very few scientists who were full-time physical anthropologists, particularly ones interested in the early phases of human evolution. Those who did respond to the discovery of *Australopithecus* were at least as dismissive as their British counterparts, perhaps more so. Physical anthropologist W. W. Howells, then a student at Harvard, later wrote: "On the American side there was, in 1925, no establishment critically equipped to assess Australopithecus one way or the other, and the sin seems to have been mere inattention. As undergraduates of those days we heard nothing about it in courses. . . . No scuttlebutt among enterprising or curious graduate students. . . . Physical anthropology was not yet much of a discipline, and the only real teacher was Earnest Hooton at Harvard, who was himself largely self-taught, following his own interests."[32]

Earnest A. Hooton was born and raised in Wisconsin, where he received an undergraduate degree in the classics from Appleton College. As a Rhodes Scholar at Oxford in 1910 he was introduced to anthropology by Robert Marrett, and was later influenced by Arthur Keith. He returned to the United States in 1913 and began a lifelong tenure at Harvard University teaching physical anthropology, at the time not a part of most anthropology programs in America. According to Harry Shapiro (1981), during the time when he was Hooton's first graduate student, there were "less than half a dozen recognized physical anthropologists in the United States."

Hooton was predominantly interested in the application of physical anthropology to modern society, but he occasionally wrote on human evolution. All he had to say in describing the fossil evidence from Africa was: "A form of anthropoid ape has recently been discovered at Taungs, Bechuanaland, in deposits which may be of Pliocene date. This specimen, which has been named Australopithecus africanus, displays, according to some writers, affinities with gorilla and chimpanzee. At any rate it demonstrates the presence in the Ethiopian area of a hitherto unknown type of anthropoid ape belonging to a geologically ancient horizon."[33] Again, the fossil was that of an ape—thereby eliminating in many scientists' minds the possibility that it was a hominid—and a few years later, in the first edition of the influential *Up From the Ape,* a book written for a popular audience, Hooton all but ignored Dart's fossil. In the chapter entitled "Fossil Ancestors," he wrote that the earliest known hominid, *Pithecanthropus,* "well deserves the title 'missing link.' " The only mention of *Australopithecus,* later in the same chapter, was in the context of itemizing various higher primate fossils from Africa, including "Australopithecus, alleged to be a humanoid ape of the Pliocene."[34] *Australopithecus* is completely absent from the accompanying primate family tree. He hypothesized that humans arose, perhaps more than once, during the Miocene: "It is difficult to avoid the conclusion that of the diverse families and genera of giant anthropoids developed in the Miocene period, several may have taken to the ground in different areas and at various times. Some of these attained a semi-human status and some achieved complete humanity. . . . If the finds of fossil man hitherto brought to light mean anything at all, they mean that nature has constructed many and varied experiments upon the higher primates, resulting in several lines of human descent, all of which probably issued from a generalized and progressive family of giant anthropoids not earlier than the Miocene period."[35] Nowhere is there a better example of the teleological perspective on the evolutionary process common for the time. The allusions to progress are explicit, and the idea that humans could arise more than once is obviously orthogenetic. If humans were the desired, even necessary, goal of the evolutionary process you would expect to see them evolving independently of one another.

Another prominent American physical anthropologist was Czech-born Ales Hrdlicka. In 1925 he was head of the physical anthropology division at the Smithsonian Institution in Washington, D.C., and the editor of the *American Journal of Physical Anthropology,* which he had founded in 1918, and where he remained chief editor until 1942.[36] Although Hrdlicka's main line of research involved studies of aboriginal American populations, he had written a number of papers on early humans in the Old World (Hrdlicka 1916, for example).

Aside from Broom and Dart himself, Hrdlicka was the only scientist who studied the actual fossils before commenting on their significance. Between March and October of 1925, while on a world tour examining human fossils and sites, he arranged for a short side trip to Taung while in Rhodesia studying the Broken Hill remains. The result of his three-day stopover in Johannesburg was a short paper in the *American Journal of Physical Anthropology,* which described the site and the fossils. Overall, his impression was very similar to that of the British establishment: "The find is unquestionably one of great interest and scientific importance, for it extends the field of anthropoid apes in Africa far to the south where no trace of such apes was known or expected before. . . . The skull itself is that of an anthropoid ape approaching rather closely in size and form the chimpanzee; but in all probability it is a new species, if not genus, of the great apes. . . . Just what relation this fossil form bears, on one hand, to the human phylum, and on the other to the chimpanzee and gorilla, can only be *properly* [italics mine] determined after the specimen is well identified, for which are needed additional adult specimens."[37] A completed manuscript of this paper exists which is virtually identical to the published version except it does not include the word "properly."[38] It seems as if Hrdlicka was implying that the relationship of the specimen to other forms had to date been *improperly* determined.

Various other published and unpublished records from 1925 confirm this conclusion. Soon after returning to the United States, he wrote to Dubois: "I also visited the site of the Rhodesian man as well as that of the Taungs find in South Africa and bring some interesting new evidence. As to the Taungs skull it is simply that of a fossil anthropoid ape and has, so far as I can see, no special claim to be in the direct line of man's evolution."[39] He also sent a letter to

Elliot Smith: "Dart and Drennan [an anatomist from Capetown] . . . are still young and energetic workers from whom with good help much may be expected. . . . But they need intellectual outside help and stimulation."[40] His correspondence with Woodward and Sollas from 1925 made no mention of the fossil at all, which confirms that he was not overly impressed with *Australopithecus*, or with the South African scientists themselves.[41]

In 1928 another American scientist, Gerrit Miller, a mammologist at the Smithsonian, wrote a paper in which he attempted to shed some light on the controversies surrounding what were popularly called human "missing links." Miller suggested that these transitional forms could be defined three different ways: "(a) races of men which had not lost all their ape-like peculiarities, (b) races of apes which had begun to take on human characteristics, or, (c) races which were neither exactly men nor exactly apes but which combined the characteristics of both."[42] To qualify as a "missing link," a "find" would have to show that it was part of a creature that had some of the essential characteristics of both humans and apes.[43] But Miller warned that "likeness without relationship is usually called 'parallelism' or 'convergence,' and it is so common throughout nature that everyone who is occupied with the classification of animals must be constantly ready to take it into account."[44] This belief that parallelism was "so common throughout nature" was, of course, consistent with the concept of orthogenesis. If evolution were goal-oriented, it should not be surprising to have the same structures evolving more than once. In the case of human evolution this presented a convenient way to dismiss any likeness between an "ape" such as *Australopithecus* and modern humans.

Regarding which of the existing fossil forms fit his definition of a true missing link, Miller maintained that: "As the result of 70 years of effort these tireless workers have made exactly two 'finds'—no more —which are of such a nature that they can be seriously regarded as furnishing the looked-for direct evidence of man's blood relationship with animals resembling in some general manner the present-day gorilla and chimpanzee."[45] Predictably, these two finds were *Pithecanthropus* and *Eoanthropus,* and Miller gave extremely detailed summaries of the controversy surrounding each of the fossils. However, based on his definition of a missing link, particularly what he labeled as (b), it is curious that *Australopithecus* failed to at least get a passing mention.[46]

One exception to the overall American position on *Australopithecus* was provided by zoologist H. H. Wilder of Smith College. In an attempt to erect a more uniform taxonomy for the primates based on standard zoological methodology, Wilder not only discussed the anatomy of different species, but also gave a wealth of historical information regarding nomenclature in an effort to establish priority (Wilder 1926). Among the many suggested revisions given, he proposed that anthropoid apes and humans be subsumed into a single family, the Hominidae. This was a fairly bold move at the time, but it is noteworthy that he maintained the traditional dichotomy at the subfamilial level between the great apes (the Ponginae) and humans (the Homininae). Despite giving an excellent explanation of the inherent incongruity between phylogeny and a static taxonomy based on extant forms,[47] he nonetheless fell into the gradistic trap by stating, "In this book . . . the word *apes* will refer to the *lower* [italics mine] members of the Hominidae."[48]

To Wilder's credit, he was the first person to formally classify the newly discovered Taung fossil with other fossil humans, a step that even Dart was unprepared to take: "Another extinct transition form, perhaps even more important than *Pithecanthropus,* has been recently discovered in Bechuanaland by Professor Raymond Dart of Johannesburg. It has been named *Australopithecus africanus,* and is an immature specimen, representing a child of six. As we may place both *Pithecanthropus* and *Australopithecus* within Sub-Family 3,

Homininae, further study of both will be reserved for the next chapter."[49] In that next chapter, entitled "Fossil Men," he justified his position by using an in press analysis by Elliot Smith that emphasized the humanlike traits of the face and neurocranium. Furthermore, in quoting Broom, Wilder stated his agreement with the placement of the Taung fossil, but also demonstrated the very common, and certainly orthogenetic, view that the "main line" of evolution was toward *Homo sapiens:* "The new transition form from Africa, *Australopithecus,* is evidently a little lower than *Pithecanthropus,* and nearer the direct line of human pedigree. A recent article by Broom constructs a new phylogenetic tree in which *Australopithecus, Eoanthropus,* and *Homo sapiens* lie along the main stem."[50] On his own phylogeny Wilder placed *Dryopithecus* at the node at which the Homininae and the Ponginae diverged, but for unknown reasons he left *Australopithecus* off of his human branch.

Dart and Broom also received some welcome support from William King Gregory at the American Museum of Natural History in New York. Gregory was an expert in the evolution of mammal dentition and the leading proponent of the idea that humans had evolved from some brachiating apelike ancestor. During the late 1920s he published a series of articles critical of current theories suggesting that humans did not have an anthropoid ape ancestry. In particular he took issue with the writings of his friend, and boss, Henry Fairfield Osborn (Gregory 1930a, b; Osborn 1930).[51]

In 1927, Gregory took issue with the idea that simple parallelism could account for *all* similarities between apes and humans: "It has been suggested, by myself and others, that some of the characters common to man and one or more of the anthropoids may well be due to 'parallelism,' that is, to the independent acquisition of similar characters after the divergence from a common stock; but in view of the many positive agreements the burden of proof must rest upon those who would class all of the resemblances as 'parallels.' "[52] In the

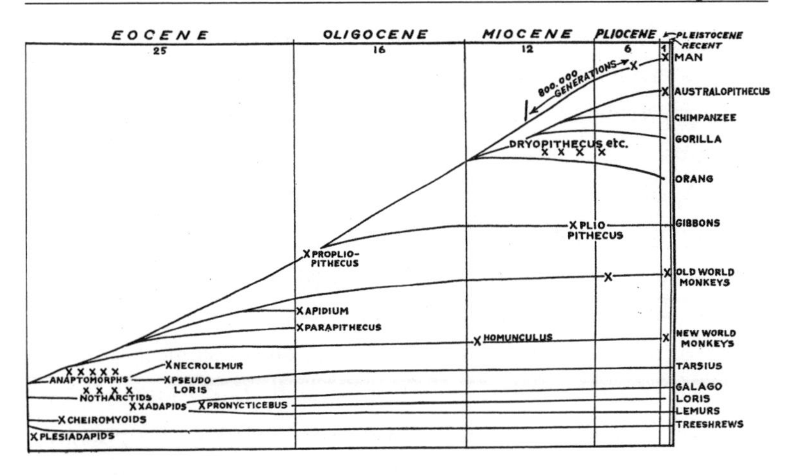

Fig. 4.4—Gregory phylogeny (Gregory 1927b, p. 559).

same publication, although no mention is made of *Australopithecus* in the text, Gregory placed the species with the apes on his phylogeny (Fig. 4.4). He later became a vocal supporter of *Australopithecus* as a human ancestor, but at this point he accepted what had become the conventional wisdom, that it was simply an ape with no connection to the human lineage.

Gregory changed his position on *Australopithecus* when Dart sent him photographs of the chewing surfaces of the teeth, newly exposed upon further preparation during October of 1929. In a letter to Dart thanking him for the new information Gregory wrote: "Upon my return from Africa I was delighted to find upon my desk your letter and the wonderful photographs of the dentition of *Australopithecus*. Dr. Hellman and I were going over them yesterday and we were astounded at its 'human-like' characters. We look forward with great eagerness to the publication of your memoir and I predict that many of those who have dismissed *Australopithecus* as just another anthropoid will be discounted in the opinion of those best qualified to judge impartially."[53] Gregory was evidently at odds with those who saw the dental resemblances between *Australopithecus* and modern humans as the result of parallel evolution. For him the teeth were evidence of a genuine phylogenetic relationship with later hominids.

In April 1930, at the inaugural meeting of the American Association of Physical Anthropologists, Gregory presented a paper outlining the most detailed account to date of his attack on Osborn's "dawn-man" theory. He dismantled Osborn's argument point by point, bringing to bear gross anatomical, embryological, and paleontological evidence in support of his own conclusions. He later wrote of the meeting to Dart: "At the anatomists-anthropologists' meeting I exhibited slides from the two photographs of the palate and the mandibular arch, which you had formerly sent me. Doctor Hrdlicka gave his usual reaction of excessive conservatism and caution. It is a 'state of mind.' "[54]

The published version of Gregory's address contained only one brief mention of the Taung fossil: "The fossil anthropoid Australopithecus has a skull and brain cast of progressive anthropoid type, but its dentition is prevailingly human. It therefore adds weighty evidence both for the close relationship of man to the gorilla and chimpanzee and for the 'brachiation' theory of human origin."[55] He had originally intended to publish more about *Australopithecus* in the article in the *American Journal of Physical Anthropology*, but Hrdlicka made it clear that this would be a detriment to the rest of his paper: "Your paper and you [*sic*] whole work is of such value to all of us that I am anxious in the most sincere friendly way that there should be nothing in your paper that might weaken it. It would do no harm to publish on the Australopithecus whatever you might wish in a separate form. In the present connection, however, I am afraid of a possible weakening by this inclusion of your otherwise very solid points of view."[56]

Another publication based on the same AAPA address appeared

soon after in which Gregory included this more detailed discussion of *Australopithecus*. After careful examination of the newly exposed chewing surfaces of the teeth, Gregory tabulated that of twenty-six dental characters, *Australopithecus* was more similar to humans than to apes in twenty, which led him to conclude that "if Australopithecus is not literally a missing link between an older dryopithecoid group and primitive man, what conceivable combination of ape and human characters would ever be admitted as such?"[57] That Gregory had completely changed his position on Taung since 1927 is clearly shown in an unpublished phylogeny from late 1930 (Fig. 4.5).[58] In stark contrast to the family tree he had constructed in 1927, *Australopithecus* is now shown as an early branch off of the already established human stem.

While Gregory was emerging as Dart and Broom's main supporter in the United States, back in England Keith published what at the time was probably considered the last word on the Taung specimen (Keith 1931). In *New Discoveries Relating to the Antiquity of Man,* Keith devoted six chapters (eighty-one pages) to the topic of *Australopithecus*. His initial query reflected his gradistic viewpoint: "The discovery of Australopithecus has carried debate to the lower threshold of the missing-link zone. Had this extinct being crossed the lower threshold and become an ape-like man, or was it to be relegated to the lower zone—to be placed with manlike apes or anthropoids?"[59] For Keith, ascertaining the ape or human status of the fossil was the initial step in determining where it should be placed on the family tree. If the specimen was shown to be an ape, not having "crossed the lower human threshold," then it simply could not be placed on the human lineage no matter how far down: "A close examination of all the features of the Taungs skull—the size and configuration of the brain, the composition of the cranial walls, the features of the face, the characters of jaws and teeth and the manner in which the head was hafted to the neck—leave me in no

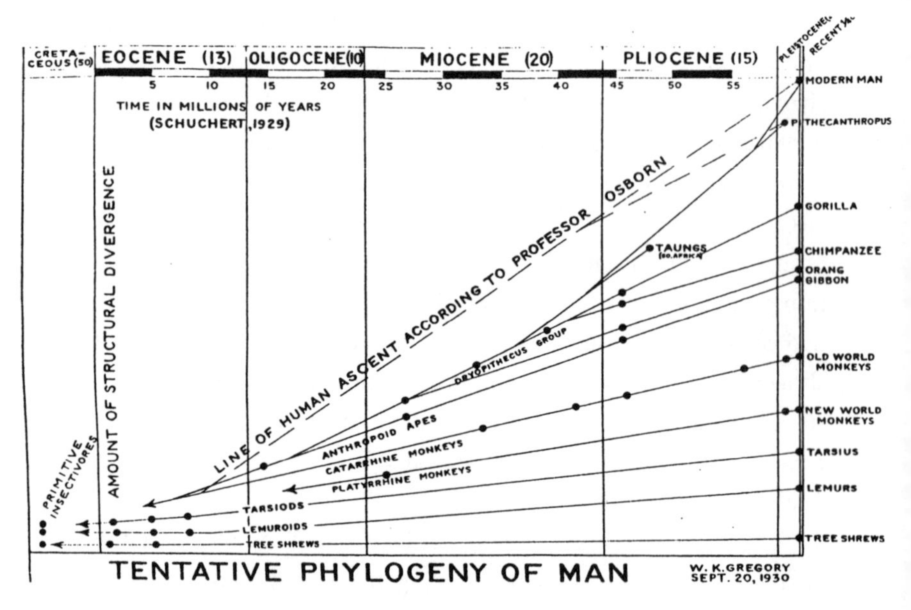

Fig. 4.5—Gregory phylogeny (unpublished 1930, Correspondence with Gregory 1924–, Hrdlicka Collection, National Anthropological Archives).

doubt as to the nature of the animal to which the skull formed a part; Australopithecus was an anthropoid ape."[60] Keith's sense of where *Australopithecus* fit within higher primate phylogeny was made plain in the family tree included in his new book (Fig. 4.6). The Taung species was shown diverging from the line leading exclusively to the chimpanzees and gorillas sometime in the early Pliocene and terminating in the early Pleistocene.

In 1933, fellow English anatomist Solly Zuckerman published a book outlining some of the difficulties of defining the relationships among living and extinct primates. Like Wilder, he was especially critical of anatomists who did not adhere to normal zoological practices, suggesting that: "Primate material has a peculiar power of overweighting the conclusions of its students. . . . Whether we like it or not, almost every fossil primate form, at least in the first excite-

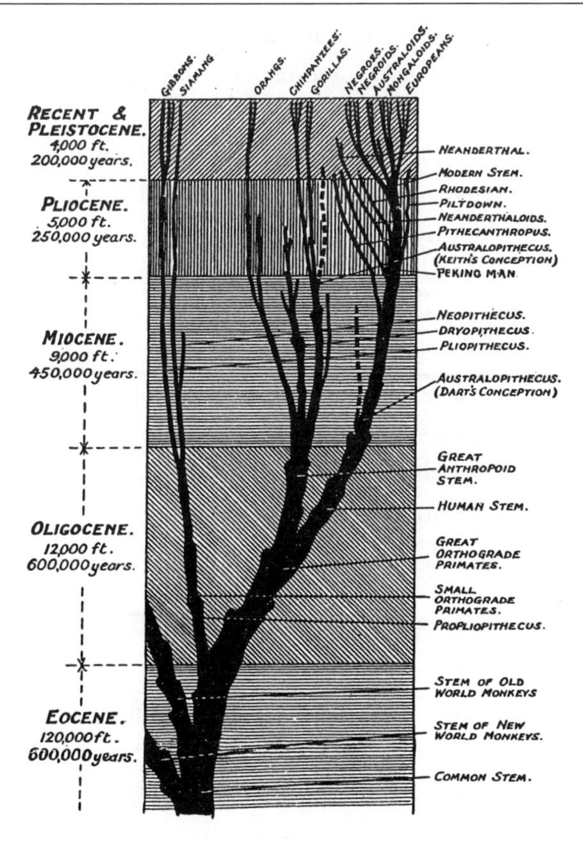

Fig. 4.6—Keith phylogeny (Keith 1931, p. 2).

ment following its discovery, is given some special significance in the story of man's descent (e.g. the Taung's fossil)."[61] While maintaining that "man's phyletic relationship with the *Pongidae* cannot . . . be seriously questioned,"[62] Zuckerman felt it was impossible to tell which species humans were most closely related to, since "it is possible that the common ancestors of the group transmitted to their descendents certain evolutionary potentialities"[63] such that the explanation for some similar traits "might well be parallel and orthogenetic evolution within the confines of a natural sub-group."[64] As with Keith, Zuckerman was quite willing to attribute certain physical similarities to parallel evolution in the direction of *Homo sapiens*.

Meanwhile, yet another English scientist, paleontologist A. T. Hopwood, felt compelled to weigh in on the Taung fossil. Hopwood described fragmentary remains of three new fossil primate genera from the lower Miocene site of Koru, in Kenya. In his summary he placed the new species in the larger context of higher primate evolution. The stem species for later Old World anthropoid evolution was *Propliopithecus*, an Oligocene monkey from the Fayum site in Egypt. *Propliopithecus*, "or something closely resembling it," was the ancestor of all higher primates in the Old World, and "those forms which went south [from the Fayum during the Oligocene] gave rise to the modern African anthropoids. Their stock also provided the unprogressive *Limnopithecus*, the aberrant *Xenopithecus*, and the precocious *Australopithecus*, but these branches from the main stem lead nowhere."[65] With regard to the latter species Hopwood quite specifically concluded that "indeed, there is very little difference between the Gorilla and *Australopithecus*, which appears to be a precocious offshoot of the gorilline lineage."[66] The perception remained that *Australopithecus* was no more than an interesting ape species, perhaps a somewhat unique form, but an ape nonetheless, and one having nothing to do with our own ancestry. Once again we see the orthogenetic idea of a "precocious" offshoot, an evolutionary failure, separate from the main stem leading toward humans.

Near-Humans in the Far East

Whatever interest in *Australopithecus* the single fossil from a remote South African location may have generated was soon overwhelmed by spectacular finds from China and later Java. The fossil record for human evolution was quite paltry when *Australopithecus* was discovered, but this situation began to change over the next few years.

For decades after Dubois's initial discovery in the early 1890s, no other early fossil hominids had been recovered in the Far East.[67] Beginning in the late 1920s, however, a series of fossil remains were recovered from the site of Zhoukoudien, in China.[68]

When Dart finally had the opportunity to bring the actual Taung fossil to Europe for the first time, he not only had to overcome the initial criticisms leveled at his interpretation of the fossil, but he also had to compete with these new fossil finds from China. Dart presented Taung to the Zoological Society of London on February 17, 1931, with the expectation that he would finally receive the accolades that up until that point had eluded him. Unfortunately for Dart, on the same day he was to present, Elliot Smith exhibited casts of the Zhoukoudien fossils in a much more polished presentation, completely overshadowing Dart and his now six-year-old discovery (Dart and Craig 1959).[69]

Dart had also brought with him his monograph on the fossil, which he hoped would be published by the Royal Society. However, not only had Keith devoted a large portion of his most recent book to *Australopithecus,* but German anatomist Wolfgang Abel had just published a lengthy monograph of his own on the Taung baby (Abel 1931). In this paper Abel, like Keith, concluded that *Australopithecus* was nothing more than an interesting extinct ape species. Consequently, the Royal Society decided to reject Dart's monograph, agreeing to publish only the part on the dentition. Dart refused, saying that it was all or nothing, although he eventually did publish the part of his memoir on the dentition in a much more obscure periodical (Dart 1934).

Beyond Taung

Between November 1924 and July 1936, only the single type specimen of *Australopithecus africanus* was known to science. Most modern writers tend to focus on the fact that during this ten-year period there was a relative dearth of interest in the Taung remains. While this is true relative to the number of publications surrounding other fossil material, especially from the Far East and Europe, it is perhaps more remarkable that the Taung infant held the interest of the scientific community to the extent that it did. After all, Dart's find was the only one of its kind, it was of uncertain geological age, it was a juvenile, and there were no elements preserved from the postcranial skeleton. For instance, Columbia University anthropologist Ralph Linton wrote in 1936: "This skull is, unfortunately, that of an infant, and some of its manlike characteristics may be due to this fact. . . . Eoanthropus and Pithecanthropus had attained completely erect posture and were probably constant ground-dwellers, while for the Taungs species the evidence is not negative but lacking."[70] In his discussion of *Australopithecus* James McGregor expressed what had become the conventional wisdom regarding the South African species: "Professor Dart believes that the creature walked upright, but there is nothing in the skull to warrant this or to indicate that its balance on the spinal column was essentially different from that of a young chimpanzee. On all discussions of Australopithecus it is important to keep in mind that the skull is that of a very young individual and that no other part of the skeleton is known. It exhibits a remarkable mixture of simian and human features and is beyond question the most manlike of known anthropoid apes, but this special manlikeness may well be an example of parallelism."[71] Accordingly, in his family tree McGregor placed *Australopithecus* as an offshoot of the lineage leading to the extant African apes.

For the vast majority of scholars in England and the United States the Taung debate was for the most part over with. A consensus had formed by 1936 as to the pattern of human evolution. The human lineage had sprung from some Miocene ape ancestor, represented by *Dryopithecus* and the numerous genera and species from the Siwaliks.[72] Pithecanthropus and *Sinanthropus* were viewed as the most primitive humans, and the increasingly enigmatic Piltdown, along with other "archaic" *Homo sapiens* (e.g. Mauer, Steinheim, Broken Hill, and Swanscombe), were regarded as undoubtedly human, although their exact relationship to modern *Homo sapiens* was equivocal.

Discussion of what the earliest humans looked like, and when and where they appeared, remained vague. This was partly because most scientists were still making a grade distinction between humans and "other," and did not differentiate between the categories of human and hominid. For a species to be included as human it had to meet certain anatomical requirements, such as a certain brain size, fully erect posture, and so forth. In most people's minds, these same requirements held for inclusion in the Hominidae. Hence, it was impossible to count *Australopithecus*, or any other apelike creature, among the Hominidae. Until a clear distinction was made between classification based upon grades and phylogeny based on clades, only fossils bearing a close resemblance to modern humans could be included in the Hominidae and placed near them on a family tree.

Though future events would show that *Australopithecus*, or something very similar to it, was a direct human ancestor, with the lone fossil from Taung as the total evidence it does not seem unreasonable that many researchers at the time were skeptical. However, new fossils collected beginning in 1936 by Robert Broom would once again focus attention on South Africa, and once again call into question preconceptions about the appearance of our earliest ancestors.

Born and raised in Scotland, Robert Broom was a physician by trade, but with a strong interest in paleontology. After receiving his master of surgery degree from Glasgow University in 1889, Broom moved to Australia, where he practiced medicine from 1892 to 1896. During this period he received his doctorate from Glasgow for his comparative analysis of the organ of Jacobson. This analysis led to an interest in the evolution of the Mammalia from some reptilian ancestor, and in 1897 Broom moved to South Africa, a region where numerous early "mammal-like" reptiles had already been found. He subsequently named and described many new species of these reptiles that he recovered from the Karroo region in South Africa, and in 1920 he was rewarded with membership to London's Royal Society.[73]

Although his work on the evolution of the Mammalia was widely known, his interest in paleoanthropology took root fairly late in life. He wrote a few brief papers on the essentially modern Boskop skull discovered in South Africa in 1913 (Broom 1918, 1925c, 1926), and had an interest in the various living groups of indigenous South Africans. He was an early and enthusiastic supporter of Dart's contentions regarding the Taung fossil (Broom 1925a, b, 1929, 1930a, b, 1934), and upon his retirement as a physician and his appointment to the Transvaal Museum in Pretoria, South Africa, in 1934, he became fully involved with paleontological work. After a year and a half working on fossil mammal-like reptiles, he wrote, "in May [of 1936] I thought I would begin to hunt for an adult Taungs ape."[74] One of the initial criticisms of Raymond Dart's interpretation of *Australopithecus* was that it was based on the remains of a juvenile. This point was rendered moot in 1936 with the discovery of the type specimen of *Australopithecus* (later *Plesianthropus*) *transvaalensis*. This adult cranium, and additional fossils collected in the Sterkfontein Valley by Broom over the next five years, slowly rekindled interest in the South African "ape-men."

After searching for several weeks in the numerous limestone caverns and caves dotting the countryside around Pretoria[75] without any success in finding adult *Australopithecus* remains, Broom visited a site called Sterkfontein on the recommendation of two of Dart's students, H. le Riche and G. W. H. Schepers from Witwatersrand.[76] Schepers and le Riche showed Broom the fossil remains of baboons they had found at Sterkfontein, and Broom, like Dart before him, asked the foreman, a man named Barlow, who had worked at Buxton and had seen the original Taung fossil, to keep an eye out for anything similar. A mere eight days later Broom received the first new *Australopithecus* fossil since Dart's discovery in 1924: "On the Monday following, August 17, 1936, I was again at Sterkfontein, and when I saw Barlow, he handed me a beautiful brain-cast, and said, 'Is this what you're after?' I replied, 'Yes, that's what I'm after.' "[77] The following day Broom returned and found more pieces of the same individual Barlow had discovered. In all, the specimen consisted of a crushed partial cranium, including the right upper jaw with several teeth, and most of a natural endocast of the brain (Broom 1936a, b, c) (Fig. 4.7). Broom named his new fossil *Australopithecus transvaalensis,* recognizing its similarities to Dart's fossil, at least regarding the few common skeletal parts, yet seeing enough difference to warrant a species distinction. He estimated the brain size from the endocast as 600 cc, and noted that although the canine itself was missing, the alveolus suggested that the tooth was quite small. Based on the fauna, which differed from that of Taung, indicating to Broom a younger age, he said, "The Sterkfontein deposit is most probably Upper Pleistocene." As for the phylogenetic placement of the new fossil, Broom was a bit vague in his brief article in *Nature:* "The discovery shows that we had in South Africa during Pleistocene times large non-forest living anthropoids—not very closely allied to either the chimpanzee or gorilla but showing distinct relationships to the Miocene and especially to the Pliocene species of *Dryopithecus*. They also show a number of typical human characters not met with in any of the living anthropoids."[78] In a popular article published concurrently with the *Nature* article he was a bit more forthcoming: "Not improbably it was from one of the Pliocene members of this group [represented by the Sterkfontein and Taung fossils] that the first man was evolved."[79] After further preparation, in October Broom sent a second short article to *Nature,* describing

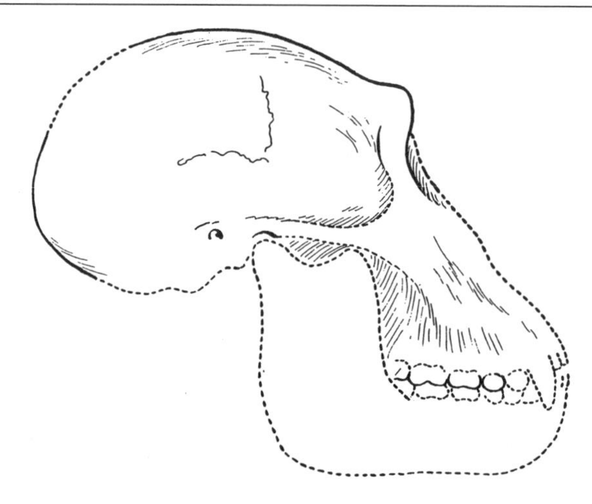

Fig. 4.7—Broom's reconstruction of the type specimen of *Plesianthropus transvaalensis* from Sterkfontein (Broom 1936b, p. 477).

another feature of his new fossil that resembled humans more than any living ape. He noted that there was no diastema, or gap, between the upper canine root and adjacent incisor tooth root on the newly discovered left side of the upper jaw. This corroborated Dart's similar statements regarding Taung.

Even while emphasizing the human qualities of *Australopithecus*, Broom repeatedly stated that his fossil was that of an ape, as had Dart, yet one that was certainly not allied with extant apes, and one that showed some definite affinities with humans. In fact, in a gradistic sense, *everyone* classified the South African species as apes, which for most experts mandated their placement along with the extant apes, the Pongidae, on the primate family tree. Broom, however, believed that numerous dental similarities, especially in the milk dentition, indicated an actual genealogical connection, and placed *Australopithecus* on the line toward humans despite its characterization as an ape (Broom 1936c).

Yet Broom continued to undermine his own position by concluding that "one might describe *Australopithecus* as a chimpanzee with human teeth." This statement was interpreted by others as confirmation of a fundamental ape morphology with one or two oddly human features. As he had done previously, Broom published a concurrent popular account describing his new fossils: "We need not at present discuss the exact position of *Australopithecus,* but we can without any hesitation state that here we have an anthropoid ape with a brain capacity of probably between 450 and 650 cc, *and thus definitely an ape* [italics mine]. Perhaps the transformation of a prehuman type like *Australopithecus* into a primitive man came about fairly rapidly through the development of a large brain. But how the change came about is still mysterious. Was it a chance mutation, or a mutation arising from some directing spiritual force?"[80] Such metaphysical statements in a scientific forum were not uncommon for Broom, yet this could not have helped change the minds of many already skeptical people.

Paranthropus robustus

Since one of the main criticisms of Dart's fossil had been its young biological age, it might have been expected that the scientific community would have had a strong interest in Broom's new fossils. However, the Sterkfontein fossils did not generate the high level of attention that Dart's original announcement had over a decade earlier. In the only comment to *Nature* on the new finds, after dismissing arguments that both the Sterkfontein and Taung specimens displayed humanlike qualities, Dr. Ernst Schwarz of London concluded: "The fact that Dr. Broom's specimen does not represent an ancestral form of the hominoid line does not detract from the extreme value of the discovery. It is to be hoped that he will be able to continue his researches, and to elucidate the history of anthropoids in Africa, an undertaking quite as important and interesting as that of the ancestors of man himself."[81] It is hard to imagine a more condescending tone, which further fueled Broom's cynicism toward the English scientific elite.

The fact that the new fossils from Sterkfontein did not convince the scientific community did not forestall Broom's ongoing research. In June of 1938 he arrived at Sterkfontein on one of his routine visits and was presented with an upper jaw by Barlow. Immediately recognizing differences between this new fossil and the existing Sterkfontein material, Broom pressed Barlow on the provenience of the new specimen, and was informed that the palate had not actually come from Sterkfontein, but had been obtained from a local schoolboy. Broom tracked the boy down, and was shown the spot on top of a small hill where the fossil had been found. The new site was about two miles from Sterkfontein, and was called Kromdraai, after the farm where the hill was located. Upon further searching, Broom and his assistants recovered much of the left half of the cranium and the right side of the mandible. As before, he quickly sent off announcements to the popular press as well as to *Nature,* giving a preliminary description of the new material (Broom 1938b, c). He emphasized the numerous differences between his new fossil and *Australopithecus,* especially in the morphology of the second premolar and canine, but also in features of the cranium, suggesting that the new species was even more humanlike than was *Australopithecus*. Based on these differences he not only erected a new species, but also made a generic distinction, referring the Kromdraai specimen to *Paranthropus robustus:* "Herewith is a short account of a wonderful new find. It is the nearest approach to man yet discovered, and I feel sure it will be universally accepted as the 'missing link.' . . . [The find is] of even greater importance than the Taungs or the Sterkfontein specimens."[82]

He also took the opportunity based on further finds and analyses of the Sterkfontein specimens to present a new genus name for them as well: "The shape of the symphysis [displayed by "the incisor portion of the jaw of a young male"] is so different from that of the Taungs ape that it seems advisable to place A. transvaalensis in a distinct genus, for which the name Plesianthropus is proposed."[83] The following year he added: "The brains [of the Taung and Sterkfontein fossils], however, differ markedly in shape, and I have thought it advisable for this and some other reasons to put the Sterkfontein ape in a distinct genus, *Plesianthropus*."[84]

Broom's publications unequivocally show that he continued to view the South African species as representative of a group that had given rise to later hominids in a phylogenetic sense. However, whether he realized it or not, he was asking a different question when trying to determine if the South African forms were to be classified as human. As a subscriber to Darwinian evolution he recognized that primitive, nonhuman (apelike) forms had to be a part of our ancestry. A letter to W. K. Gregory in New York illustrates Broom's thinking: "My Paranthropus is I fancy going to have a brain of over 600 cc. Will let you know in a few weeks. If it proves to be 650—Is it a Man? If Koenigswald's Pithecanthropus is a Man with 750 cc—Where are we to draw the line?"[85] Broom was clearly aware that the distinction between man and ape was an arbitrary one, and he also understood that one or the other of the South African species could be ancestral to later hominids *regardless* of their grade status. This was a critical distinction that was lost on many other members of the scientific community, who equated grade statements with phylogenetic ones.

The great majority of the debate surrounding the South African fossils concerned the anatomy of the skull and teeth. Questions about the role that bipedalism played in the evolution of humans became more prominent with the discovery of postcranial elements. Broom had previously alluded to the fact that the South African apes were "more erect" than any living ape based on the morphology of the basicranium: "Part of the hinge on which the skull is supported is preserved [in the *Paranthropus* type], and is situated farther forward than in living apes, a point suggesting that the new fossil form walked in a more erect posture."[86] Dart had made a similar argument based on the anterior position of the foramen magnum of the Taung specimen. Soon after the discovery of *Paranthropus,* Broom described postcranial elements of the type specimen, including an upper arm bone, "from which we may infer as probable that Paranthropus, like man, was a bipedal animal, and that the arms were not used for locomotion, but for the manipulation of sticks and possibly tools."[87] In the same publication he also discussed newly discovered postcranial elements from Sterkfontein presumably belonging to *Plesianthropus:* "The [distal] femoral fragment seems to indicate that *Plesianthropus* was also probably a bipedal animal."[88] This paper is of some interest for two other reasons that reflect Broom's iterative approach to his subject. He again revised his estimates of cranial capacity, based on information derived from the recovery of new remains. In an anonymous abstract of Broom's article, mention is made of these new estimates, and the emphasis on grade classification based on brain size is in this case fairly obvious: "The brain cast, when reconstructed, would place the capacity of the brain of *Plesianthropus* next in the scale of measurement, so far as at present known, to the recently discovered specimen of *Pithecanthropus* from Java.[89] Pithecanthropus, no longer in danger of being classed as a gibbon, is definitely *above the human border-line* [italics mine]."[90]

In December of 1938, J. C. Middleton Shaw of the University of the Witwatersrand discovered in the Sterkfontein Valley, not far from Broom's sites, an upper left third molar "which differs in many respects from, but yet has certain characters of the same order as, those revealed by some of the upper molars of *Plesianthropus transvaalensis* and *Paranthropus robustus*."[91] Broom later responded that the single tooth was likely from one of the species he had already described: "Though there are differences in this tooth from the other two described [upper third molars from Sterkfontein attributed to *Plesianthropus*] it seems to me that it approaches more closely even to the type tooth than it does to any known human tooth, and that it is more likely to be a Plesianthropus tooth than a human tooth."[92] The question again arises of what issue is being addressed here. In 1941 anatomist A. J. E. Cave stated that Shaw's fossil may be "of hominid rank and hence the earliest human fossil found," clearly reflecting a view of hominid and human as equivalent categories. Broom, on the other hand, viewed his fossils as undoubted apes, yet on or very close to the lineage leading directly to modern humans.

W. K. Gregory's Visit to South Africa

W. K. Gregory was considered the leading expert in the evolution of the mammalian dentition, and he spent considerable time and effort concentrating on the human dentition in particular (Gregory 1916, 1922; Gregory and Hellman 1926). He supported Darwin's theory that humans had evolved from some nonspecialized Miocene anthropoid, such as *Dryopithecus*, and concluded his 1916 monograph on the evolution of the primates as follows: "Comparison of the upper and lower molar patterns, both in the deciduous and permanent series, furnishes clear evidence that man is nearly allied to the Mid-Tertiary genera *Sivapithecus* and *Dryopithecus* and more remotely to the existing Chimpanzees and Gorillas."[93] Similarly, in his 1922 volume on the human dentition he summarized his position on the phylogenetic relationship between humans and other primates: "The conclusion indicated by the foregoing review of the dentition and to which all the rest of my investigations have also led, is that the Hominidae have been derived from the Dryopithecus group of the

Simiidae in the late Tertiary. This conclusion is supported by the concurrent testimony of comparative anatomy, which as will presently be shown, points to a very near relationship of the Hominidae to the gorilla-chimpanzee division of the Simiidae."[94] Throughout the late 1920s and into the 1930s Gregory continued to focus on the anthropoid ancestry of humans, often in articles attacking the position of those who suffered from what he called "pithecophobia," especially H. F. Osborn and F. Wood Jones. In 1930 he concluded that *Australopithecus* was just the type of creature that structurally would bridge the gap between apes and humans, even if it did not represent a direct ancestral link.

In March of 1938 Gregory received an invitation from Broom to come to South Africa to study all of the original fossils. Broom wrote: "You can examine on the spot all the Australopithecus finds and you will be at liberty to express any opinions you form, whether they confirm or contradict those of the local workers."[95] Broom must have assumed he was on fairly safe ground, since he and Gregory had a long-standing professional relationship. At a reception for Gregory upon his arrival in South Africa Broom said: "W. K. Gregory and I have been in almost constant correspondence for over 30 years. We have been almost like brothers. We have discussed almost all sorts of technical questions in connection with evolution and I have always found him to agree with me very closely."[96] Gregory had arranged Broom's lecture tour across the United States a year earlier and was instrumental in Broom's reception of an honorary doctorate from Columbia University. Broom was well aware that Gregory had previously written in favor of *Australopithecus* as a possible genetic link between extinct apes, such as *Dryopithecus*, and early humans, such as *Sinanthropus*. Gregory also received an invitation from Dart to come and examine the Taung specimen in Johannesburg. Along with colleague Milo Hellman he spent the better part of July and August in South Africa, carefully studying the original specimens in Pretoria and Johannesburg, and making casts and taking photographs to take back to New York.

The papers he subsequently published placed Gregory squarely in the debate over the interpretation of the fossils, a position he was well suited for considering his earlier papers on the evolution of the human dentition. By December, Gregory and Hellman had completed their analysis and sent a detailed manuscript to South Africa to be published in the *Annals of the Transvaal Museum*. They also sent a letter to Dr. H. R. Raikes, the chairman of the senate at the University of the Witwatersrand: "You may be interested in our general result, which is a confirmation of Dr. Broom's conclusion that the extinct South African man-apes are structural links between the families of apes and men."[97]

While their full analysis was being prepared for publication, the two scientists sent brief notices to both *Science* and *Nature* giving a summary of some of their most important findings (Gregory and Hellman 1938, 1939a). In accordance with previous studies of anthropoid dentition, the authors made it clear that they viewed the South African species not only as structural grades between humans and dryopithecines, but as genuine genealogical relatives of later hominids. They may have been late-surviving cousins, and not direct ancestors, but this distinction was of little consequence as far as they were concerned; here were representatives of the late Tertiary group that gave rise to humans. Even if the two authors were reluctant to define the exact phylogenetic placement of the South African fossils, they were very specific in assigning them a higher-level classification. In the title to the short notice they sent to *Science*, Gregory and Hellman referred to the South African fossils as the "australopithecine man-apes." This marks the first time that a subfamily designation was given the three genera collectively, and they were undoubtedly using the term in the same sense that Gregory had referred several related species to the Dryopithecinae.[98] They seized the opportunity to once again adamantly, and somewhat caustically, state that humans and apes were part of the same taxonomic radiation, and that theories requiring more distant hypothetical ancestors were baseless:

> In 1926 H. H. Wilder, in his excellent book, "The Pedigree of the Human Race," took the bold step of uniting apes and men in a single zoological family, the Hominidae. If mice rather than men were being classified, this would have been widely recognized as a genuine discovery, in line with the more fundamental one by Linnaeus that man is a member of the natural order Primates. But most of the clergy, innumerable educators and a vast majority of the laity can not stomach the Linnaean classification because it brackets with the "brute beasts" that self-conscious and conceited prig who calls himself *Homo sapiens* and is fond of acting like the viceroy of God. The supposed phylogenetic isolation of man is even a favorite theme of those scientists who rest their beliefs upon an uncritical acceptance of catch-words such as "polyphyletism," "parallelism," "irreversibility of evolution," and the like.[99]

Gregory, like other nonanthropologists such as Wilder, was critical of the way anatomists and anthropologists viewed the evolutionary process and pattern. He was much more interested in form and function (that is, adaptation) within groups of animals than simply naming and classifying them (Rainger 1989).

Gregory and Hellman gave a public summary of their findings in a paper delivered to the anthropology section of the American Association for the Advancement of Science in December of 1938. After listing the humanlike features of the fossils, they addressed the possible place of the species in the broader scheme of anthropoid evolution: "*Plesianthropus* presents such an astonishing mixture of ape and human characters that, for a long time, we were in doubt whether to call it a very progressive ape or a very primitive man. A third alternative is that it is an ape which has paralleled man in certain features, but this hardly does justice to the numerous features in which it is transitional between the ape and human families."[100] Despite rejecting the common orthogenetic explanation for similarities, they still succumbed to the standard practice of making a grade distinction between a primitive human and a progressive ape, again confounding clear phylogenetic interpretation. They, perhaps inadvertently, confused the critical point that the distinction between ape and human was arbitrary, and irrelevant from the point of view of phylogeny.

Gregory and Hellman's complete analysis was published by the Transvaal Museum later in 1939 (Gregory and Hellman 1939c). In it they stressed the truly mosaic nature of the fossils, with humanlike dentition, but ape-sized brains. One of the major anatomical traits of interest was the morphology of the anterior dentition, particularly the canine/anterior premolar complex, which in apes and monkeys is very distinct from that of modern humans: "From the foregoing it will be evident that both Plesianthropus and Paranthropus with their small front teeth and advanced premolars had progressed far in the human direction."[101] Hellman, a specialist in the shape of the dental arcade among the anthropoids, concluded upon reconstructing the shape of the upper jaws that "in both the adult South African apes the upper dental arch form was approaching the lower limits of the human stage."[102]

Although they combined all of the South African forms in a new subfamily, and even went so far as to state that the Homininae were "large-brained, omnivorous-carnivorous derivatives of the early australopith branch," Gregory and Hellman fell short of including the australopithecines in the Hominidae. They also did not include a phylogenetic tree as part of their analysis, which might have clarified their position. Despite these shortcomings, their general conclusion supported the position of Dart and Broom: "In conclusion, some anthropologists may regard the South African man-ape group merely as a second, later and abortive attempt of nature to evolve a human type long after she had set apart that branch which eventually won fame as evolving into *Homo sapiens*." That they would even entertain the idea that nature would make a "second attempt" at evolving humans indicates a view rooted in orthogenesis, demonstrating the powerful influence this supposed evolutionary force still held. The authors did not agree with this concept, and continued: "These South African Pleistocene man-apes were both in a structural and a genetic sense the conservative cousins of the contemporary human branch. Although it is far too much to expect that the close structural approach of *Plesianthropus* toward *Sinanthropus* will discourage those who cling hopefully to the myth of Eocene man, all the facts known to date (in contradistinction to unproved assumptions of 'irreversibility,' 'parallelism,' etc.) tend in our judgment to confirm the conclusions of Davidson Black (1925, pp. 175–9), Weinert and the present authors, who regard man as the result of a morphological revolution which took place during the late Tertiary period."[103]

The overall conclusion of Gregory and Hellman was that the australopithecines, like humans, were derivatives of the Miocene ape stock. Probably due to the recent geological age of the South African species, they did not place them in the direct line of human evolution, but, like Broom and Dart, suspected that the actual human ancestors had looked very similar to these "conservative cousins." A gradistic approach to classification must have retained some influence on their analysis, since Gregory and Hellman intentionally did not include the Australopithecinae in the Hominidae, even though they were comfortable placing the Dryopithecinae in the Simiidae.

The scientific community, again focusing on new finds from the Far East, remained skeptical. Roy Chapman Andrews, a colleague of Gregory's at the American Museum of Natural History who was famous for his dinosaur discoveries in the Gobi Desert, agreed with Gregory's assessment of a dryopithecine ancestry, but was equivocal on the matter of *Australopithecus*. In a popular book he wrote: "Apparently he [*Australopithecus*] was an attempt by nature to produce man in South Africa just as had been done at earlier times in other parts of the world. He was a non-progressive sub-human."[104] This last phrase, clearly reflecting an orthogenetic point of view, can be readily interpreted within the context of the temporalized Great Chain. With humans as the ultimate goal of evolution, *Australopithecus* was "an attempt by nature," and presumably only one of many such attempts, to evolve true *Homo sapiens*. The South African species did not achieve this goal, and was left on the threshold as a "non-progressive sub-human."

E. A. Hooton published a heavily revised second edition of his text *Up From the Ape* in 1946, in which he began his discussion of "fossil ancestors and collaterals" with a cautionary note on the use of the dentition to determine taxonomic status: "Dentitions that would have been assigned confidently to early apelike forms of man have been discovered implanted in crania of veritable apes."[105] Certainly he was speaking of the australopithecines, about whom he concluded: "Although these Pleistocene apes of South Africa are undoubtedly much closer to man than any existing or extinct subhuman forms heretofore discovered, they lacked the brain overgrowth that is specifically human and perhaps should be *the ultimate criterion of a direct ancestral relationship to man* of a Pliocene precursor [italics mine]. Because they lacked brains, they remained apes, in spite of their humanoid teeth. Since the Australopithecinae died out in Africa, while the gorilla and the chimpanzee survived, it would appear that a thorough-going ape is better than half a man."[106] Hooton was making the same error that had been made for decades. He was asserting that if the South African species did not have large brains, they had to be classified as apes. This is legitimate in a strictly gradistic sense; however, in stating that this grade distinction defined the phylogenetic placement of the australopithecines he was incorrect; as noted by Dart, Broom, and Gregory, they could be categorized as apes and still be ancestral to later humans.

Nonetheless, for Hooton and most others, the features of the australopithecine dentition and skull that seemed to foreshadow those of *Homo sapiens* were still sufficiently different enough that they could be accounted for by parallelism. The evidence for bipedalism was dubious, so there was little discussion on this point. One can imagine how the history of paleoanthropology might have been different had Dart or Broom recovered more convincing remains from the postcranial skeleton. As we will see in the next chapter, just such remains became available in the late 1940s, and helped steer the scientific community toward acceptance of the idea that human beings had evolved from a bipedal ape ancestor that once lived among the savannas and woodlands of sub-Saharan Africa.

CHAPTER 5

Darwin Redux

Despite Broom's numerous discoveries at Sterkfontein and Kromdraii and the detailed analyses of the original fossils by Gregory and Hellman, in the mid-1940s the case for the australopithecines as human ancestors was not widely accepted: "In 1946, the generally accepted view of most anatomists and zoologists was that the South African australopithecines were simply a local variant of an apelike creature similar to the gorillas and chimpanzees, and were in no way directly related to the family of man, the Hominidae."[1] Many authorities had solidified their opinion on the significance of the South African anthropoids over the previous decade based only on the Taung specimen. They felt that during the Pleistocene in South Africa there existed an interesting group of apes that displayed some curious human features, but were apes nonetheless. There existed a certain level of intellectual inertia that would be extremely difficult to overcome.

Part of the problem with the material discovered between 1936 and the beginning of World War II was that it was quite fragmentary. There were bits of jaw, isolated teeth, broken-off ends of limb bones, and so forth (Appendix A.3). Given these conditions it was difficult to establish even basic biological features such as exact brain size, locomotor pattern, or body size. What was of equal and perhaps greater importance was a continued adherence on the part of the anthropological community to archaic evolutionary principles. In fact, an emphasis on "types" or grades of hominids and related anthropoid forms led to an almost complete lack of appreciation of evolution as a process. Human and hominid continued to be mostly synonymous terms, and any fossil species that did not conform to this perceived type, usually defined by some arbitrary cranial capacity, were excluded from human ancestry. Continued acceptance of orthogenesis as a legitimate evolutionary principle allowed for the dismissal of the australopithecines and many extinct apes as parallel lineages to the "real" human line of descent.

The Modern Synthesis

Current wisdom holds that the recovery of additional fossils, particularly from the pelvis, led to the recognition of an australopithecine phase of human ancestry. What is often not considered is the changing theoretical context within which these fossils were interpreted. In the years immediately following World War II, more complete fossils *were* recovered from new and existing sites in South Africa (Appendix A.4). By the time these specimens were collected, biological studies had undergone a fundamental transformation that was later dubbed the modern synthesis (Huxley 1942, Mayr and Provine 1980). This synthesis involved field biologists, geneticists, and paleontologists finding a common ground in their previously separate investigations into the evolutionary process. The focus was on adaptation; novel variation was generated by mutation at the molecular level, which was then acted upon by natural selection, shaping the organism to fit its environment.

One of the crucial outcomes of the synthesis was that scientists began thinking in terms of variable populations, not types. Evolution was viewed more as a *process,* and while the classification of the resultant *pattern* remained important, to some degree simple alpha taxonomy lost its primacy. The discovery of new and more complete australopithecine fossils was clearly significant, but without this shift in theory their acceptance as hominids would have undoubtedly continued to be postponed. Only now, under these new theoretical circumstances, could the scientific community welcome the australopithecines, or any apelike species, into the hominid family.

Another key result of the synthesis was the elimination of the teleological approach to reconstructing human phylogeny. In other words, the idea of evolutionary progress toward a predetermined goal (that is, *Homo sapiens*) was rejected. The novel, neo-Darwinian theoretical context overcame some of the long-standing influence of the Great Chain concept, and evolution was no longer viewed as a directed process.[2] The rejection of orthogenesis eliminated the argument that parallelism could explain all similarities between apes and humans. It simply was not feasible with a materialistic evolutionary process operating on random variation to have nearly identical, detailed anatomical structures appear independently in both humans and apes.

The effects of the synthesis were not immediately felt within the anthropological community, and during the 1930s and 1940s physical anthropologists and anatomists continued to work within what had become an archaic biological context. A few hints of what was to come did exist, however. In 1940, Raymond Dart published on *Australopithecus* for the first time since 1934. While he felt compelled to leave "in Dr. Broom's hands the explanation of the sub-human fossils," he nonetheless made a few summary statements about their current status: "Although all three [australopithecine genera] are admitted to be intimately related to one another, we have still to learn whether the two more recent genera discovered by Broom are really man-like apes, or whether they have not, in point of fact, crossed the diminutive gap which separates the Australopith group proper from human status. This is what I am inclined to believe, and that Dr. Broom's specimens are the most primitive types of mankind of which we have evidence."[3] Although Dart was getting lost in the question of grade classification, this is one of the first instances, if not the first, in which anyone had referred to the australopithecines as humans in any sense. He even more clearly drove this point home by quoting Darwin: "In a series of forms graduating insensibly from some ape-like creature to man as he now exists, it would be impossible to fix any definite point where the term 'Man' ought to be used. But this is a matter of very little importance."[4]

Dart seemingly understood the arbitrariness of any definition of human vs. ape, and in stating that the question of where to draw the line between the two is of very little importance, he showed that he also understood that this question had little bearing on the separate question of phylogeny. In retrospect, I would argue that the question of where to draw the line between ape and human was paramount in the minds of many scholars, including Robert Broom.

In a study of the dentition of the australopithecines a year later, Mazaffer Suleyman Senyurek, a Turkish student studying under E. A. Hooton, published an analysis that was complementary to those of Gregory and Hellman. Like them, Senyurek concluded that: "Australopithecus, Plesianthropus and Paranthropus had evolved on quite a different line from all the known anthropoids. Also, it is certain that this is the very same line by which also man has evolved."[5] From this statement and the phylogeny figured in the paper, it is clear that Senyurek viewed the australopithecines as part of the lineage that eventually led to *Homo sapiens*. Yet despite his seemingly clear position, he asked: "Should we regard them [the australopithecines] as advanced anthropoids standing in ancestral relation to man or as very primitive hominids still retaining some ape characters?"[6] Issues of phylogeny and grade-based classification were still confounded, but Senyurek rejected the position of those who viewed similarities between humans and the South African fossils as the result of parallelism: "They possess many . . . resemblances to man which cannot be attributed to parallelism."[7] Although the typological distinction between ape and human remained, it seems as though it was becoming harder to reconcile the view of evolution as a nondirected process with taxonomic conclusions that depended on orthogenesis and parallelism.

A few years later University of Wisconsin anthropologist William Howells published a general text on human evolution called *Mankind So Far*.[8] As for the australopithecines, after listing the several characters of the teeth, skull, and postcranium that possibly linked them with humans, Howells wrote: "Now here is a pretty problem. Are these apes or are they men? Are they to be put with the Pongidae or the Hominidae?"[9] That these two questions were for so long considered the same demonstrated the lack of distinction between grade classification and actual phylogeny. However, Howells, like Dart in 1940, appeared to be one of the first to reject the synonymy of these questions: "Now, *Homo sapiens* applies purely to the modern, living type of man, and to those skeletons which, no matter how old, are unquestionably of the same kind in all details. But *Hominidae* is the name of a family and not merely of a species, and it takes in all the men who ever lived, no matter how primitive."[10] He very definitely was making a distinction between human and hominid. Perhaps just as important was his assertion, to some extent based on this distinction, that inclusion in the Hominidae had less to do with brain size and everything to do with locomotion: "Zoologists have never yet bothered to select one single feature to differentiate men from apes, one definite line to take a stand, because they were not faced with the necessity. But forced to the choice, most of them would say that man zoologically became man when he first walked erect on the ground, or at least developed an arch to his foot."[11]

Many zoologists would probably have disagreed with this statement at the time, arguing that a certain level of encephalization was required for inclusion in the Hominidae. But Howells's shifting of emphasis from the cranium to the lower limb became crucial over the next few years.

Broom's Monograph

Global political events precluded further excavation of the South African caves during World War II, but Broom kept busy by performing detailed analyses on the fossils discovered up until 1941, when excavations ceased. He published numerous short notices during the war that provided preliminary conclusions based upon ongoing work, and once hostilities ended, Broom synthesized all of the information at hand into one volume. The monograph was published in January of 1946 by the Transvaal Museum, and entitled *The South African Fossil Ape-Men, the Australopithecinae.* J. C. Smuts, who was instrumental in getting Broom involved in the search for human ancestors in 1934, wrote the preface, in which he nicely summarized Broom's general conclusion: "There lived in Africa, contemporary with real primitive man and in close proximity to him, a small-brained, partly erect-walking, cave dwelling race or races of apes (we can scarcely call them ape-men) who may have used some sort of implements, and perhaps practised some kind of speech."[12] Smuts's parenthetical comment, in which he takes issue with Broom's informal categorization of the australopithecines as ape-men, displays a continued attempt to place the fossils into the existing grade system initially designed to accommodate living forms. As far as Smuts and many others were concerned, a species had to be one or the other, and in this case he felt that ape was the more accurate category.

His comments on Broom's research on South African mammal-like reptiles further reveal an adherence to the idea of orthogenesis, or evolution as a directed, goal-oriented process: "The birds—so far from forming, as some had supposed, the intermediate link between reptiles and mammals—now appeared as a sideline off the main line of animal advance, a beautiful lateral development, now ranking among the greater glories of this world, but essentially a dead-end, by-passed by the real advance, which has moved on from the reptiles to the mammals and to man."[13] He could just as easily have been referring to the australopithecines as a "sideline off the main line of animal advance" toward humans.

The body of the monograph consisted of two main sections. Broom handled the history of the discoveries, including a running commentary on many of the contemporary articles on the subject, and also the detailed descriptions of, and conclusions based on, the skeletal and dental remains. G. W. H. Schepers, a student of Dart's, described the several cranial endocasts that had been recovered and speculated on possible behavioral implications derived from the reconstructed morphology of the brain. Dart himself would have seemed the obvious choice to undertake this particular analysis, since it was the humanlike features of the Taung endocast that initially got his attention. Yet despite expert knowledge of both neuroanatomy and the South African fossils, he was not involved in the production of Broom's monograph. Although Dart was approached to do the analysis, he turned the offer down, because, he claimed, he was too intimately involved and would perhaps be viewed as biased. An alternative suggestion comes from Broom's assistant, J. T. Robinson, who believed that Dart and Broom had very different personalities, which made working together difficult (Robinson pers. comm.). This impression is supported by the fact that the two never collaborated on a single paper.

Broom devoted one chapter to each of the three genera, describing the australopithecine fossils themselves and the associated fauna, the latter to establish the geologic age of the sites and occasionally the paleoenvironment. His final chapter, entitled "Affinities of the Australopiths," compared and contrasted the different species, and then attempted to place them in the larger scheme of anthropoid evolution. He enumerated a series of cranio-dental differences between the three forms to justify their distinction at a generic rank, but at the same time acknowledged their similarities and affirmed Gregory and Hellman's creation of a single subfamily to encompass all three.

In Broom's mind, the significance of the australopithecines had not changed much over the previous decade, and his final thoughts in the monograph were very similar to the concluding remarks he made in many of his shorter papers: "What we now know with moderate certainty is that a group of higher Primates lived in South Africa in Pliocene time and apparently survived into the Pleistocene. These primates agreed closely with man in many characters. They were almost certainly bipedal and they probably used their hands for the manipulation of implements."[14] Broom did not discuss the issue of bipedalism at any great length, but here he plainly stated that as a group they walked on two legs. He was unsure, however, to what extent their type of bipedalism was similar to that of modern humans. In comparing *Plesianthropus* and *Paranthropus*, the more anterior position of the foramen magnum in the latter led to the conclusion that "probably Paranthropus walked even more erect than Plesianthropus."[15] For Broom, and probably for others, bipedalism was not simply a matter of presence or absence.[16]

The monograph's influence on the scientific community was palpable, and positive reviews were written by various scientists including Gregory (1946), Eiseley (1946), Senyurek (1947), and Keith (1947), who conceded that his initial interpretation of the Taung fossil was no longer tenable. Broom had been in the habit of sending Keith periodic updates on his work, occasionally including casts of some of the more interesting specimens. Two years before the publication of the final monograph, Keith wrote to Broom: "No doubt the South African Anthropoids are much more human than I had originally supposed, and I am prepared to swallow plantigrade adaptations on their limb bones."[17] Of all of the humanlike features discussed over the years by Dart and Broom, it is interesting that Keith made a point of agreeing that the australopithecines were bipedal and that this perhaps clinched their human status. Although a few authors had suggested that bipedalism was the initial adaptation in the human family, it was believed that an increase in brain size soon followed or occurred at roughly the same time. Now it was becoming evident that bipedalism evolved in a lineage that maintained an apelike cranial capacity for a significant period of time.

Keith capitulated even further in his brief comment to *Nature* soon after the publication of Broom and Schepers's volume: "When Prof. Raymond Dart, of the University of the Witwatersrand, Johannesburg, announced in Nature the discovery of a juvenile Australopithecus and claimed for it a human kinship, I was one of those who took the point of view that when the adult form was discovered it would prove to be near akin to the living African anthropoids—the gorilla and chimpanzee. Like Prof. Le Gros Clark, I am now convinced, on the evidence submitted by Dr. Robert Broom, that Prof. Dart was right and that I was wrong; the Australopithecinae are in or near the line which culminated in the human form."[18] Significantly, Keith mentions Wilfrid Le Gros Clark, who over the next few years would play an enormous role in the acceptance of an australopithecine stage of human evolution.

Wilfrid Le Gros Clark

Wilfrid E. Le Gros Clark is probably best known to anthropologists for his comparative anatomical approach to the study of primate evolution and his emphasis on "total morphological pattern." He entered St. Thomas's Hospital Medical School in London at the age of seventeen, and at the end of World War I completed his studies and became a fellow of the Royal College of Surgeons at the young age of twenty-four.[19] He spent the years from 1920 to 1923 on the island of Sarawak in Southeast Asia as principal medical officer, in his leisure time doing research on the local primates, particularly the tarsier and the tree shrew, the latter being regarded by some scientists at the time as a very primitive member of the primates.

Upon returning to England in 1924 he first took a position as anatomist at St. Bartholomew's Hospital; then in 1929 he moved back to his alma mater, St. Thomas's Hospital, where he was chair of anatomy for five years. Finally, in 1934 he accepted a position as professor of anatomy at the University of Oxford, where he would stay for the remainder of his career. He became a Fellow of the Royal Society one year after arriving at Oxford, and was eventually knighted in 1955.

In addition to his impressive medical research, he published germinal work on early primates (Clark 1934), and his primate evolution textbooks became the standards, influencing virtually all students of physical anthropology for decades (Clark 1949a, 1955, 1960).[20] Early in his career, Le Gros Clark's interest in primate evolution was mainly restricted to the most ancient stages. Nonetheless, prior to his direct involvement with the australopithecines, he had written a few general papers on human evolution (e.g., Clark 1928, 1937, 1938). Like Gregory, Le Gros Clark did not initially accept an australopithecine ancestry for humans. His opinion on the South African fossils, and on an ape ancestry in general, was fairly typical for the time: "It is probable that the *Dryopithecus* group branched out into several lines, some of which subsequently became extinct. One of these lines is represented by an interesting fossil from South Africa—*Australopithecus*. This extinct ape had developed many features which were remarkably human (such as the characters of the dentition and the shape of the palate), so that some anatomists were led to suppose that it must bear an ancestral relationship to modern Man. It is evident, however, that its geological age is too recent to permit acceptance of this hypothesis. Its main interest lies in the inference that, since it was almost certainly derived from the earlier *Dryopithecus* group, the latter was apparently endowed with the requisite evolutionary potentialities for the development in the direction of the *Hominidae*."[21]

One of the main sticking points surrounding *Australopithecus* continued to be its comparatively recent geologic age. Keith, and others, had often emphasized this point even as Broom's published dates for the fossils became progressively older based on new faunal discoveries at Sterkfontein and Kromdraai. But there was another related issue that Le Gros Clark discussed in a subsequent paper: "With the discovery of a somewhat specialized gibbon, *Limnopithecus,* and a primitive chimpanzee, *Proconsul,* from the Miocene deposits in Kenya, it becomes evident that at the beginning of the Miocene the main groups of the anthropoid apes which exist to-day were already undergoing separately their evolutionary definition. The importance of this fact is related to the general belief (based on comparative anatomical data) that man and the modern anthropoid apes had their origin in a common ancestry, and that the human line of descent became first differentiated at the time when the modern genera of anthropoid apes commenced their own divergent specializations. Hence it is in the palaeontological records of this geological period that the initial appearance of the Hominidae is probably to be sought."[22] As long as it was accepted that separate anthropoid evolutionary lineages leading to extant species had already existed in the Miocene, the earliest members of the human lineage would have to be of similar age. Unless the australopithecines were shown to have existed during the Miocene, and nobody was proposing such an early date for any of the South African sites, they could not be directly ancestral. Hence in 1940 Le Gros Clark was not willing to accept *Australopithecus* as a human ancestor: "We may accept as an established fact that the teeth and palate are in several respects certainly more human than any of the living anthropoid apes. On the other hand, there is no room for doubt that these fossil genera are really apes and not primitive types of humanity."[23]

By the time Broom and Schepers published their monograph in 1946, Le Gros Clark had become a frequent correspondent with Broom, and his opinion on the australopithecines was becoming more favorable. He first became acquainted with Broom at Zoological Society meetings in London, which Broom attended whenever he was in England. They exchanged many letters during World War II, and Broom often sent updates on his research to Le Gros Clark, who eventually became an important ally in England. He wrote to Broom: "I have no doubt at all in my mind that Plesianthropus and Paranthropus represent really very remarkable discoveries, and we are sincerely grateful to you not only for bringing them to light, but for letting us have information about them in your interim publications."[24] As for Broom's critics in England, Le Gros Clark apparently shared a little of Broom's cynicism toward the British scientific establishment: "One or two people had come to acquire such a popular reputation that they seemed to be regarded almost as oracles. And unfortunately they enjoyed the role, and took it upon themselves to express far-reaching opinions based on very little personal evidence."[25] In defiance of these "oracles," even before the publication of the monograph the general opinion in England seemed to be changing. After Le Gros Clark requested photographs of the finds (Broom often sent only drawings), both casts and photos were sent in 1945 and presented to the British Association. According to Le Gros Clark: "There was a big audience for the news had got around that some of your new evidence would be presented. The pictures . . .

actually aroused applause. . . . The Anthropology section decided to send you congratulations."[26]

By the time Broom and Schepers's monograph was published, Le Gros Clark was leaning toward acceptance of the authors' main conclusion: "Dr. Broom has demonstrated beyond any doubt at all that the Australopithecinæ are extremely important for the study of human evolution, since they present an astonishing assemblage of simian and human characters. Such an assemblage, indeed, might well be postulated, entirely on indirect evidence, for the hypothetical ancestors of the Hominidæ."[27] Six years after stating that the australopithecines were undoubtedly not "primitive types of humanity," he seemed to have changed his opinion completely. Like Keith, and Howells in America, he also acknowledged that the postcranial evidence was becoming more crucial in the interpretation of the fossils: "So far, then, the Australopithecinae might perhaps be regarded as a group of extinct apes, somewhat similar to the gorilla and chimpanzee, in which the characters of the dentition had developed (possibly independently) along lines almost identical with those of human evolution. But Dr. Broom has also, in his indefatigable search, brought to light some most important fragments of limb bones, which allow, and even make probable, a much more startling interpretation of these fossil remains . . . the lower end of the femur is perhaps the most important of all the limb-bone fragments, and Dr. Broom infers from it that Plesianthropus 'walked, as does man, entirely or almost entirely on its hind feet.' "[28]

In another article published soon after his review of the monograph Le Gros Clark continued to wrestle with the seemingly contradictory interpretations derived from the small, apelike brain and the hominidlike features of the teeth and postcranial skeleton:

> The question now inevitably arises whether these fossil Primates have a direct or indirect ancestral relationship to *Homo sapiens,*

> or whether they are not rather representatives of an extinct line of apes which, in their teeth and limbs, showed an astonishing parallelism with the line of human evolution. And if the former is the true interpretation, should they be regarded as advanced types of man-like apes, or exceedingly primitive types of ape-like men? Few anatomists are likely to agree that they come within the category of "men," if only because the size of their brains was relatively no greater than that of the modern large apes, but the blend of hominid and simian characters in the teeth and limbs nevertheless remains a most striking feature. It is a matter of the highest importance that more limb-material of the Australopithecinae should be obtained for examination.[29]

Here, Le Gros Clark first asked whether or not the australopithecines had an ancestral, or phylogenetic, relationship with modern humans. Even if the answer was yes, the question of whether they should be classified as apes or humans remained to be determined. In other words, he had decoupled the questions of phylogeny and classification, with the understanding that there could be a gradistic ape in the line of human ancestry. It is also noteworthy that he again made it clear that the evidence from the postcranial skeleton was crucial in making a phylogenetic interpretation, implying that he rejected the argument that parallelism could account for *all* similarities.

When the first Pan-African Congress on Prehistory was scheduled in Nairobi for January 1947, Le Gros Clark took the opportunity to first visit South Africa to examine the fossil evidence firsthand. Despite his friendly relationship with Broom, and his favorable published statements about the role of the australopithecines in human evolution, he arrived there in December of 1946 still uncertain of his position. Recalling the events twenty years later he wrote: "I still remained doubtful of the suggestion that the australopiths were hominids rather than pongids, and I was still inclined to take the latter view. So far as the contentions of Dart and Broom were concerned, therefore, I felt I was going to South Africa as the 'devil's advocate' in opposition to their claims."[30] He had made a careful study of dozens of ape crania before leaving for South Africa, with the expectation that in examining the australopithecines he would find a preponderance of pongid features, with a few hominid traits. Upon seeing the actual fossils, however, he soon recognized that it was the hominid features that stood out:[31] "The results of my studies were very illuminating . . . because they at last convinced me that Dart and Broom were essentially right in their assessment of the significance of the australopiths as the probable precursors of more advanced types of the Hominidae."[32]

After arriving in Johannesburg in December of 1946, he spent several days staying at Dart's home and studying the Taung skull. He then headed north, where he visited the various Makapan Valley sites, and then arrived in Pretoria to meet Broom and begin studying the Sterkfontein and Kromdraai specimens. In a letter to his family back home he wrote: "I work all day in the museum studying the fossil apes. And extremely interesting they are! In fact, it is worth coming out here just to see them alone. They are really *most* remarkable—but I won't go into anatomical details in this letter!"[33] Even though he still referred to the fossils as apes, he clearly did not see what he had expected going in, suggesting that even upon initial examination he was impressed by the hominid features and/or the lack of affinity with the living apes he had so closely studied before leaving England.

In addition to studying the fossils, on New Year's Eve, Le Gros Clark had the opportunity to drive out and see the australopithecine sites for himself: "Yesterday, David [Evans, an astronomer whom Le Gros Clark was staying with in Pretoria] brought Broom and myself over to J'burg, and we reached Dart's home by 10:00 A.M. Then Dart, Broom and I set off on an expedition to visit some of the sites where the fossil apes have been discovered—Sterkfontein & Kromdraai. They are about 40 miles west of J'burg—not far from Krugersdorp. We also went to another place called Gladysvale about 14 miles further on, where Broom has found a new cave with very rich fossiliferous deposits."[34]

Le Gros Clark's opinion on the significance of the australopithecines was rapidly changing, and over the next three or four years he would do more than perhaps any other person to shape the conventional wisdom about our earliest ancestors.

The First Pan-African Congress on Prehistory

After several years of preparation, Louis Leakey convened the first meeting of the Pan-African Congress on Prehistory, in Nairobi, Kenya, during January of 1947 (Leakey and Cole 1952). The timing of the event was auspicious in that Le Gros Clark had just completed his survey of the South African fossils, and attended the congress while en route back to England. Broom and Dart were also in attendance.

Broom gave a brief account of the history of the discovery of the australopithecines, and made his view unusually clear: "There can be no doubt that Dart's discovery of Australopithecus has opened a new chapter in our knowledge of human origins. It was the first discovery of a family of pre-men, from some member of which man as we know him almost certainly arose."[35] Perhaps feeling extra confident with the weight of Le Gros Clark's opinion behind him, Broom, although still making the gradistic distinction of "pre-men," placed the australopithecines directly in the line of human ancestry, something he had been reluctant to do in the past.

In his address to the congress, Le Gros Clark concurred with Dart and Broom's conclusions.[36] He rejected the possibility that the detailed resemblance of the australopithecines to later hominids could be the result of parallel evolution. He listed eight anatomical regions in which the South African fossils resembled hominids more than apes, but rather than view them separately, he emphasized the need to consider the total morphological pattern. The idea of examining an organism as a whole was very influential, since many scientists had been in the habit of basing their phylogenetic and taxonomic conclusions on only one or two isolated characters: "If all the facts enumerated above are taken into consideration (and it is of the utmost importance that they should *all* be considered together as components of a total pattern) . . . [then] the Australopithecinae represent an extinct group of the Hominoidea which must be associated with the line of hominid evolution rather than with that leading to the modern large apes."[37] Still, it is revealing that the papers by Broom and Le Gros Clark were presented as part of the "Symposium on Fossil Apes in Africa," and not as part of the "Symposium on Fossil Man in Africa" held two days later. This may have reflected Leakey's bias, since he never really accepted the australopithecines as bona fide hominids until Mary Leakey discovered the remains of a species similar to Broom's *Paranthropus robustus* at their own site of Olduvai Gorge in 1959.[38]

Upon returning to Oxford from Nairobi, Le Gros Clark set to work on his full analysis of the South African fossils. The tone was set right in the first paragraph of the resulting paper, where he provided two reasons that justified the writing of another major paper on the australopithecines so soon after the appearance of Broom and Schepers's monograph: "It has now become apparent that the fossils are of quite paramount importance in relation to problems of human phylogeny, and it is, therefore, hardly possible to overemphasize their significance. . . . It has to be admitted that, in the past, several anatomists of recognized distinction have, by their misinterpretation of the evidence, tended to belittle their importance."[39] His report summarized much of what had already been published on the dentition and the skull, but it contained a much more detailed section on the postcranial remains than Broom had presented. The bones from the limbs, and particularly the lower limb, had become paramount in Le Gros Clark's thinking. Upon completion of his detailed analysis, he rejected the possibility that parallel evolution could explain the australopithecines' numerous similarities with Hominidae, and finally stated the logical conclusion that others had implied, but had not explicitly stated: "Finally, the more detailed knowledge of Australopith anatomy which is now available demands a careful reconsideration of the taxonomic status of these extinct hominoids. It seems clear that while in their cerebral development, and therefore in the *general* proportions of the skull, they represent a level of evolution corresponding to that of the large anthropoid apes, they show no structural evidence of close relationship to the latter. On the contrary, the advanced characters which are already very evident in their skull, dentition and limb bones indicate their position in the phylogenetic radiation of the Hominidae rather than the Pongidae."[40] Without using the modern jargon, Le Gros Clark was making a statement consistent with the current taxonomic philosophy known as cladistics. The "advanced characters" he described as linking the australopithecines with the other known Hominidae would today be referred to as shared derived traits, or synapomorphies. Based on his own firsthand knowledge of the fossils, Le Gros Clark arrived at a conclusion that is "modern" to the extent that it seemed to overcome the grade-based taxonomic classification of old, and included apes as early members of the hominid radiation.

Back to Sterkfontein

After the long hiatus in excavation due to the war came to an end, Broom resumed fieldwork in early 1947. After three months at Kromdraai failed to produce any significant australopithecine fossils, he returned to Sterkfontein in April. As before, good fortune was his, and he was almost immediately rewarded with some of the most complete and important specimens collected to date. In June of 1947 he discovered a fairly well preserved lower jaw, together with part of the upper jaw, and part of a shoulder joint, probably all from the same individual. The lower jaw conclusively showed that the canine was worn in a human fashion, from the tip down, very unlike that of an ape (Broom and Robinson 1947a). This was especially important since it was suspected to be a male jaw, in which the canine would presumably be larger than in a female. Broom estimated that the cranium that would have matched the mandible would have had a capacity of around 650 to 700 cc. It is not likely that a truly reliable estimate could have been generated from the available remains, but Broom had preconceptions that, if not fully supported, at least were not negated by the new fossils.

In August he recovered a nearly complete edentulous, but undistorted, cranium of *Plesianthropus* (Broom 1947), which later became known as "Mrs. Ples." The specimen was considered to be female based on the small socket associated with the missing canine tooth. Perhaps the most important fossils collected since the resuming of excavation were the bones from a partial skeleton also obtained in August of 1947 (Broom and Robinson 1947b). Specimen STS-14, which Broom suspected was a female, consisted of numerous vertebrae and ribs, parts of the femur and tibia, skull fragments, and, most important, a nearly intact pelvic bone (Fig. 5.1). Based on the lower limb bones Broom gave rough stature estimates of four feet tall for females and five feet tall for males.

The pelvis was clearly more human than apelike, making this the most convincing evidence for bipedal locomotion yet recovered. Le Gros Clark, in describing all of the new finds from 1947, stated that the "os innominatum . . . is without doubt the most remarkable find. . . . It provides the final proof . . . that the Australopithecinæ stood and walked in approximately human fashion" (Clark 1948a). He must have received word from Broom almost immediately on the new find, since he sent a letter dated August 9 off to Keith in which

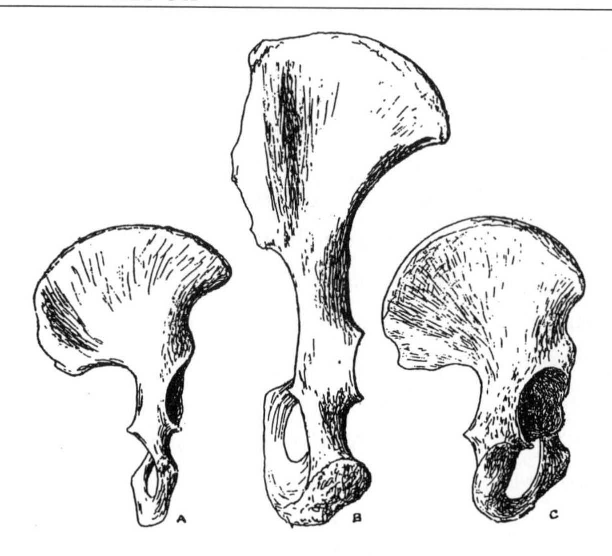

Fig. 5.1—A: Pelvic remains of *Plesianthropus transvaalensis* Broom discovered at Sterkfontein in August 1947; B: chimpanzee; C: modern human (Broom, Robinson, and Schepers 1950, p. 60).

he wrote: "I am sure you will like to hear the news (which I have just received from Broom) that he has got practically the whole skeleton of Plesianthropus, which he found in direct association with the skull and mandible. So the evidence is now fairly complete, and it bears out in a remarkable way the inferences already drawn from the earlier and less perfect material. The pelvis is particularly instructive. The os innominatum (the right side of which is complete) is entirely human in its general proportions."[41] These new finds fired Broom's enthusiasm further, and he became emphatic in his phylogenetic placement of the australopithecines: "The conclusion to which some of us have come, namely, that man has evolved from an Australopith of Pliocene times, seems likely to be proved to be correct."[42] No longer was he talking of late-surviving members of the early human stock, or evolutionary cousins. As far as he was concerned, these fossils represented the direct ancestors of later hominids.

Dart Strikes Again

Over the next few years, numerous corroborating specimens were recovered at Sterkfontein, including another knee joint, a second male lower jaw, and several partial crania (Broom, Robinson, and Schepers 1950). In addition, during the late 1940s many fossils were collected on and around a farm called Makapansgat, about two hundred miles north of Johannesburg in the Central Transvaal. There are several caves in the area that had been known for many years; in fact Raymond Dart had known of prehistoric sites in the region as early as 1925 (Dart 1925c). Broom had also visited the area in 1936 and recovered a new bovid species at a cave site that was named Buffalo Cave in honor of this discovery.

Fossils were first collected at what was known as the Limeworks site in 1945, by students from the University of the Witwatersrand (Tobias 1997). Faunal remains extracted from this area indicated that the site was older than other caves and outcrops in the region, and therefore might contain remains of *Australopithecus*. As was the pattern with both Taung and Sterkfontein, fossil monkeys were discovered first, which generated further interest in the Limeworks site, and in September 1947 James Kitching found the occipital region of the skull of an australopithecine (Dart 1948a).

Raymond Dart officially reentered the picture in May of 1946, when he accompanied one of the student expeditions to the Makapan Valley. At the first Pan-African Congress, held prior to Kitching's discovery, Dart presented a paper in which he discussed the various sites at Makapansgat, particularly the Limeworks site, at which he had found fossil bones he suspected had been burnt in fires created by australopithecines. In prose typical of Dart he stated: "The Makapansgat valley limeworks fire-middens indicate that the South African man-apes were hunters of large game in terrifying possession of Heraclean club, Samsonian jawbone, and Mowglian firebrand; unless speech was also a barrier, they are separable from man only by the intellectual wall that was finally breached by implements of stone."[43]

Dart continued to try to find novel links between the australopithecines and humans. In a volume published by the Royal Society of South Africa commemorating Broom's eightieth birthday, he presented a new analysis of the original Taung infant in which he attempted to demonstrate certain developmental features that were more human than apelike. For one thing, he noted that the milk dentition was heavily worn by the time the first adult molar erupted.[44] He interpreted this observation as follows: "The advanced stage of dental attrition in the infantile *Australopithecus* thus showed that in this important quality, protracted infancy, the australopith group made one of its most momentous steps forward in the human direction.... These infantile processes, initiated in *Australopithecus,* were concurrent with a humanoid delay in the downgrowth of the face, a humanoid backward rotation of the face relative to the forwardly-expanding brain capsule and a resultant humanoid downward inclination of the orbital aperture."[45]

Dart attributed this protracted infancy to the process now generally referred to as heterochrony, which is defined as changes in the timing or rate of development of certain features. In the case of *Australopithecus,* the changes involved a general retardation in growth and development that resulted in the retention of juvenile features in adult individuals: "Thus *Australopithecus* declares his near relationship to mankind by the degree to which he exhibits as a human forerunner the features of infancy: what van Baer (1828) called 'paedogenesis,'" Kollman (1828) 'neoteny' and Garstang

(1922) and more recent authors 'paedomorphosis' (vide Gregory 1946)."[46]

Le Gros Clark also contributed a paper to the Broom volume, in which he examined differential rates of evolutionary change in individual anatomical complexes within the primates. In this paper he very succinctly explained the nature of the confusion surrounding the australopithecines over the last twenty years:

> It also seems probable that students of human evolution had been unduly influenced by a conception that the primary factor in the development of hominid forms from simian ancestors was the expansion of the brain, the suggestion being that it was this expansion which, by conferring a greater aptitude for muscular skill and a greater capacity for enterprise in the search for new environments, led to the adoption of terrestrial habits and an erect posture with a consequent modification of the anatomical structure of other parts of the body. But the discovery of the *Australopithecinae* now makes it clear that this was evidently not the sequence of events in the evolution of the Hominoidea. For these fossils give quite definite evidence of a phase of evolution in which the dentition and limbs had already approximated to a hominid condition while the brain (in its size and general proportions) was still at a simian level of evolution. Once this fact is realized, the allocation of the *Australopithecinae* to their true zoological position becomes much less a matter of doubt.[47]

It is evident here that Le Gros Clark had developed a clear understanding of the mosaic nature of human evolution, and had spelled out the basic sequence of events leading to modern humans: bipedalism and the human dentition had evolved first, then the evolution of the human brain followed. This was a crucial breakthrough, allowing the traditional grade barrier between apes and humans to be breached. Only now could the South African fossils be formally classified as early hominids. One year later Le Gros Clark did just that, at the end of the fifth William Smith Lecture he delivered to the Geological Society of London, on October 19, 1949: "The importance of the Australopithecinae in connexion with problems of human evolution is now generally recognized, but it will no doubt be some time before the full significance of these astonishingly primitive hominids (as I think they must now be termed) is recognized."[48]

Meanwhile, at Makapansgat, during July of 1948, one of Dart's assistants, A. R. Hughes, dislodged a piece of breccia that contained the mandible of an adolescent *Australopithecus prometheus* (Dart 1948c). Dart had created a new species name for the Makapan fossils, based on his belief that the species was capable of making and using fire. More cranial fragments and teeth were discovered later in 1948, including a cranio-facial fragment containing some of the maxillary dentition (Dart 1949a). Very soon after, two parts of an adolescent pelvis were recovered, which Dart suspected came from the same individual as the previously described mandible. Based on the new morphological and presumed archeological evidence,[49] Dart believed he had discovered a species even more human than any of the other australopithecines: "It [the pelvic morphology] further vindicates, by its closer approximation to the human form than the *Plesianthropus* innominate bone from Sterkfontein, the foregoing evidence that *Australopithecus prometheus* walked more erectly than *Plesianthropus* and had a body build and carriage closely comparable with that of the living Bushman."[50]

Makapansgat was not the only new australopithecine site discovered after the war. In November 1948, in association with a fifteen-month expedition carried out across Africa by the University of California, Broom and Robinson began investigating a new site called Swartkrans, which was also in the Sterkfontein Valley, but about a mile from the main Sterkfontein quarry. Soon after, they recovered two upper incisors, an upper canine, and part of a lower jaw of a species that looked very similar to *Paranthropus robustus*. Since the teeth were a bit larger than those from Kromdraai, Broom named it *Paranthropus crassidens,* with the mandible as the holotype (Broom 1949a).

After part of a second maxilla was recovered, which Broom thought was from a female, Robinson collected a second, even larger mandible in 1949 while Broom was in England to be awarded the prestigious Wollaston Medal of the Geological Society of London.[51] Upon studying photographs of the new specimen, Broom wrote to *Nature* that "[one] remarkable feature about the jaw is that it has a rudiment of a chin." Robinson also had collected part of the face and palate along with the mandible, from which Broom determined that the brain must have been "very large. . . . It seems improbable that the brain can have been less than 800 cc."[52] Upon returning to South Africa Broom sent a notice to the *Illustrated London News* with photographs of the new specimens and discussed another new fossil cranium, of a juvenile. For the first time he contemplated in print the possible human status of one of the australopithecines: "The fact is our ape-man [from Swartkrans] is in structure so man-like that the question arises, ought we not to call him early man?"[53] Previously he had stated that the new Sterkfontein specimens led him to the conclusion that the australopithecines were directly ancestral to later hominids. Now he was suggesting that not only were they ancestral in a true phyletic sense, but that they should be designated as the most primitive member of the human grade as well. This possibly reflects his retention of the synonymy of the terms human and hominid. In order to claim hominid status for his fossils, he would have to prove that they were human, which might explain his questionable observation of a rudimentary chin. It could also be that he was reacting to Dart's claims that the Makapan species was more human than the others.

Broom suspected that the Swartkrans site was older than the other sites, with the possible exception of Taung. Despite the presence of an australopithecine species allied with the one from Kromdraai, which he had thought was the most recent of the three original sites, he wrote that the Swartkrans assemblage might "prove to be much older than the Sterkfontein, possibly Upper, Middle, or even Lower Pliocene."[54] Until the very end of his life, Broom thought in terms of grade distinctions, and he apparently was suggesting that *Paranthropus crassidens* might make a better human ancestor than other australopithecines, who all had smaller cranial capacities: "With a brain well within the human range it seems impossible to deny human status to the Swartkrans ape-man, and as he is clearly allied to the smaller-brained *Australopithecus* we seem to have at least two well marked stages in the evolution of man."[55] Yet in a paper published a mere three months later he stated: "*Australopithecus* and *Plesianthropus* have remarkable milk pre-molar teeth. Man has exactly the same type. But *Paranthropus* has a more primitive type, so that it seems more probable that man (*Homo*) has evolved from a *Plesianthropus*-like type than from *Paranthropus*."[56] It is difficult to reconcile these two seemingly conflicting opinions, but what is clear is that Broom did not heed Le Gros Clark's admonition to study the total morphological pattern. It is not surprising that Broom and Robinson came to conflicting conclusions by basing interpretations on single characters. Judging from the brain size of *Paranthropus*, it made a reasonable human ancestor. However, based on the morphology of the deciduous premolars, *Plesianthropus* was a more likely ancestor for later hominids. Broom's emphasis on single traits, and his strict gradistic approach to phylogeny, led to at least one awkward observation: "If size of brain is to be the main criterion for distinguishing ape and man we think the Swartkrans male being can put in a claim to be considered as possibly man, even if his female with a brain of 700 cm^3 must be considered an ape. . . . [However,] we have an interesting jaw of a female. Unfortunately it is imperfect, but it has most of the symphysis well preserved and it has a very distinct chin. . . . Perhaps the female Swartkrans being . . . may be able to put in a claim for human status by virtue of her having a human chin."[57] The ambiguities in his text are somewhat resolved by virtue of a phylogeny published as part of a popular article in 1949. Of the various australopithecines, *Plesianthropus* is shown as the closest to the later hominids (Broom 1949d).

Cold Spring Harbor

By 1950, a large number of australopithecine fossils had been collected from five different South African sites, and three of these sites were still being actively excavated. However, the most important anthropological event of 1950 did not involve describing particular fossils or discovering new fossil sites. Instead it involved a gathering of eminent scientists—including anthropologists, geneticists, paleontologists, and traditional field biologists—at Cold Spring Harbor, Long Island, for a symposium on the origin and evolution of humans (Warren 1951). Several germinal papers presented at this symposium effectively sounded the death knell for the "old" physical anthropology. The adoption of a view of the evolutionary process in line with that of contemporary biologists and geneticists, coupled with a much-improved fossil record, resulted in a sort of coming of age for paleoanthropology.

The adoption of the evolutionary synthesis by paleoanthropologists led to a number of significant changes, including thinking in terms of populations and removing the problematic concept of orthogenesis. Perhaps most important, problems with nomenclature, which were at least partially responsible for the confusion between phylogeny and classification, were recognized and began to be eliminated. Organisms were not grouped together strictly on a typological basis, but classified together as part of the same adaptive lineage. And since typology was replaced by an appreciation for populational variation, natural selection, which relied on such variation, reemerged as the most potent evolutionary mechanism.

The need for such a symposium was spelled out in the foreword to the collected papers published the following year: "In our century, the development of genetics, which studies the phenomena of heredity and variation, has caused a gradual drawing together of biological and anthropological research. . . . Nevertheless, until recently there has been relatively little contact and collaboration between anthropologists and geneticists or other biologists. The chief aim of the fifteenth Symposium on Quantitative Biology was to help establish such collaboration."[58] It was evident that the australopithecines would play a key role in the part of the symposium relating to the evolutionary development of humans: "The human species has descended from prehuman ancestors, which in some respects resembled living apes and monkeys. Much progress has been made in recent years in studying these prehuman and early human forms, owing to the discovery of a large number of extremely interesting fossil remains in several countries, particularly South Africa."[59]

Much of the symposium addressed issues of modern human variation, but two of the nine sessions dealt with the fossil record for human evolution. The first session was entitled "Origin of the Human Stock," and comprised papers by Adolph Schultz, an anatomist; George Gaylord Simpson, a paleontologist and theorist; and Sherwood Washburn, an anthropologist who organized the meeting along with geneticist Theodosius Dobzhansky. The chairman of the session was William Howells, also an anthropologist.

Schultz's paper was a general summary of his own research in primate comparative anatomy. Based on adult morphology, but also on developmental similarities, the paper concluded that it was no longer reasonable to suggest that humans belonged to any group other than the Hominoidea. After discussing numerous detailed ways in which ape and human skeletons resembled each other to the exclusion of monkeys and prosimians, he addressed the more difficult question of phylogeny: "In other words, on the catarrhine family tree man branched off in one direction somewhere very near where the Hylobatidae branched off in an opposite direction and this before the orang-utans had become committed to their specialized course and, certainly, long before the recent African apes had emerged as distinct forms. From this towering, fruitful stem of the primate family tree there must have sprouted continuously many more twigs, now dead, of which some may well have grown parallel to, or even from the branch for man. Such a former twig, quite likely, had produced the extinct australopiths."[60] The tree metaphor remained a powerful one, but now the tree had many more branches, many of which left no descendants. Notably, Schultz, like many of his contemporaries, thought that humans had diverged fairly early on, before the divergence of the great apes. He was uncomfortable placing the australopithecines in *Homo sapiens'* direct ancestry, allowing only that they may have represented a twig "even from the branch for man." However, he did emphasize that the initial adaptation on the human lineage involved habitual bipedalism: "The first and decisive specialization of man—erect, bipedal locomotion—would never have been possible had it not been prepared for by his remote progenitor, who had endowed the apes as well with at least the potentiality of the erect position. . . . It seems not at all unlikely that some of these preparations for the upright posture had become more pronounced in a few fossil anthropoids than in any of the surviving forms of apes."[61]

Unlike Schultz's data-laden presentation, Simpson's contribution was theoretical in nature. In a discussion of basic evolutionary principles he took the opportunity to emphasize that strides made in the understanding of the evolutionary process either were not heeded by anthropologists or were unknown to them: "There is hope for a repayment on the debt, but at present anthropology is more a consumer than a producer of historical biological principles. There may at times even be a certain reluctance or ineptness in this consumption."[62] Simpson also criticized some anthropologists for extrapolating well beyond what was scientifically justifiable given the often scrappy paleontological evidence available to them: "In passing, I may say that a prudent paleontologist is sometimes appalled at the extent of restoration indulged in by the anthropologists, some of whom seem quite willing to reconstruct a face from a partial cranium, a whole skull from a piece of the lower jaw, and so on."[63]

Like Schultz, Simpson did not wholeheartedly accept the australopithecines as direct human ancestors. In fact, in 1945 Simpson had published a detailed classification of the Mammalia in which he chose to place the australopithecines within the Pongidae, not the Hominidae. Although he acknowledged the presence of certain humanlike characters, he viewed the australopithecines as related to humans only in a structural sense, not a true genealogical sense. For Simpson, they provided a sort of model for what the "real" intermediate form might look like: "*Australopithecus*, together with *Plesianthropus* and *Paranthropus* which seem to me only subgenerically distinct, at most, has been considered everything from a direct ancestor of man to merely another sort of chimpanzee. Dart's placing of Australopithecus in a family 'Homo-simiadae' (1925) only served to exemplify the total ignorance of zoology so common among the special students of these higher primates (although, of course, Dart's work is excellent in his own field). I accept the opinion of Gregory and Hellman that *Australopithecus* represents a line of dryopithecines that evolved more or less in the same direction as man but did so more slowly, resulting in a structural, but not phylogenetic, intermediate stage between man and the surviving great apes."[64] It is quite clear from these passages that Simpson had little regard for anthropologists, and their seeming misuse or even ignorance of basic evolutionary theory. It is also evident that Simpson continued to think gradistically in implying that there even *could be* an intermediate phylogenetic link "between man and the surviving great apes." Simpson also piggybacked on Gregory and Hellman's equivocation on the hominid status of the australopithecines. However, the latter scientists, if pressed, probably would have agreed that the South African species, or something very much like them (if a bit older geologically speaking), were phylogenetically related to *Homo sapiens*.

As for the principles under discussion, Simpson, like Le Gros Clark, understood the mosaic nature of evolution, and believed that based on living forms alone you could not be sure of the order in which modern features had appeared: "The same parts may evolve in different directions in different related lines, and different parts may evolve at different rates within the same line. There is thus no reason in principle why the brain may not in some cases have reached a *Homo*-like status before the lower jaw or why some primates may not have retained an ape-like brain after *Homo*-like posture was attained."[65] In the second sentence he is certainly referring to Piltdown and the Australopithecinae, respectively, and acknowledging that at least in theory, either scenario was possible in evolving humans from some apelike ancestor. What is apparent, however, is that the timing and order of the appearance of distinctive human traits was still not satisfactorily resolved in Simpson's mind. Additionally, not all anthropologists accepted bipedalism as the first essential adaptation in human development, although the STS-14 skeleton certainly went some way in swaying the scientific community. While it may have been possible to accept similarity in the dentition as the result of parallelism, the idea that bipedalism could arise twice was perhaps too improbable. Anthropologist Sherwood Washburn of the University of Chicago later said: "In the skull and dentition, there are features that definitely suggest evolution in the direction of man. These serve to strengthen and corroborate the evidence of the pelvis, but, taken by themselves, they would scarcely be sufficient to prove a close relationship."[66]

Although Simpson was a bit vague on the exact phylogenetic status of the australopithecines, his main contribution came from his analysis of how evolution worked with regard to process. He attacked the principle of orthogenesis, which was often encountered in discussions of the relationship between humans and other primates: "Orthogenesis is so firmly established as a paleontological principle among non-paleontologists that a paleontologist called in to discuss the theories of his profession generally feels that he cannot leave the subject out. . . . Practically every recent special study of the subject concludes that there is no such thing as orthogenesis. . . . Almost all authorities agree that trends are adaptive and are guided by natural selection."[67] I have included relatively more text from Simpson's short paper because in no other publication are the roots of the confusion surrounding the australopithecines more clearly defined. As one of its architects, Simpson obviously had a very firm understanding of the modern synthesis. This view, which led to his criticism of physical anthropology, demonstrated that scientists outside of the field were aware of problems that escaped the anthropologists themselves. The recognition of these problems, mainly by a younger group of formally trained, full-time anthropologists, finally allowed the discipline to "catch up" with the rest of the biological sciences.

Sherwood Washburn was one of the new anthropologists. His contribution at the Cold Spring symposium illustrated how the new generation of physical anthropologists was influenced by the evolutionary synthesis, and how this influence translated into a new understanding of the process of human evolution. He had previously written a review for the *American Journal of Physical Anthropology* of a new volume entitled *Genetics, Palaeontology, and Evolution*, edited by two of the symposium's contributors, E. Mayr and G. G. Simpson, along with G. L. Jepsen. In his review, he summarized the current definition of evolution according to biologists (*sensu lato*), which "differs very materially from that now current in physical anthropology, especially in the following ways: (1) The unit of study is the population, and emphasis is on adaptation. (2) The type specimen is no longer of paramount importance and typing a selected group of individuals out of a population is not permissible. (3) Using a few supposedly non-adaptive characters is not considered a proper way to trace phylogeny. (4) Evolution may and does reverse. (5) Apparent orthogenesis is due to a long-continued selection in one direction."[68] Here Washburn hit on virtually all of the main points that others, including Gregory, Le Gros Clark, and Simpson, had discussed as criticisms of various human evolutionary models. If basic changes in the biological sciences were lost on most anthropologists, Washburn could not be counted among them.

At the symposium, Washburn's introductory paragraph provided a very straightforward summation of the changes that were occurring in the study of human origins: "There are three reasons why this is an appropriate time to discuss the origin of man. The first is the finding of abundant fossils of a new kind of missing link in South Africa. The man-like apes indicate an unanticipated stage in human evolution which radically alters all current theories of human origins. The second reason is that, through the work of numerous geneticists, zoologists, and paleontologists, a theoretical framework is now available which is far superior to any previous evolutionary theories. The third is the fact that evolutionary speculations can be experimentally checked to a far greater extent than has been realized in the past. It is the combination of new facts, new theories, and new hopes of proof which makes this an auspicious moment to reconsider the problem of human origins."[69] Here he nicely encapsulates the main thesis of this present work; that it was a combination of new fossil discoveries interpreted within a new theoretical paradigm that led to the recognition of *Homo sapiens*' African ape ancestry. Even Washburn, however, could not completely eliminate the old language regarding grade distinctions: "There is no gap in the record [of the dental evolution] at all, and, on the basis of molar teeth, one would have an exceedingly difficult time in deciding where apes left off and man began."[70] Still, for Washburn, and perhaps most of the participants at the conference, while the question of ape or human may have had some relevance for discussions of adaptation, it was meaningless in terms of reconstructing phylogeny. Put simply, the direct ancestors of humans at one time were apes regardless of where the line was drawn between the two.

Like Schultz, and an increasing number of scientists, Washburn saw the pattern of evolutionary change within the Hominidae as beginning with the transition to bipedalism: "In summary, the critical primary adaptation initially responsible for the origin of man as a distinct group is in the pelvis. . . . Changes in the teeth, brain size, and many other parts of the body took place at a much slower rate and continued on into late Pleistocene times."[71] He now saw human evolution as a truly mosaic process, in which rates of change varied according to which anatomical complex was being studied. The resultant phylogenetic reconstruction had the australopithecines placed firmly at the root of the human lineage.

Regarding classification, Washburn agreed with Le Gros Clark that the hominid family must include all of the members of that lineage, no matter how different from the only living species they might appear. And now, inclusion in the Hominidae was based on the bipedal adaptation exclusively: "If the term 'family' is reserved for a group of animals representing a major adaptive radiation. . . . Within the human family one genus, *Homo,* might easily include all the Pleistocene large-brained hominids (Java man, Pekin man, etc.). One other genus, *Australopithecus,* might contain the man-apes (*Aus-*

tralopithecus, Plesianthropus, Paranthropus, and perhaps *Meganthropus* and even *Gigantopithecus*)."[72]

If his presentation at the Cold Spring Harbor symposium foreshadowed the future of paleoanthropology, Washburn's most elegant synopsis was delivered one year later, to the New York Academy of Sciences. Here, he formally referred to the transformation in human evolutionary studies in the title of his presentation, "The New Physical Anthropology," a phrase that would be embraced by much of the anthropological community: "The new systematics is concerned primarily with process and with the mechanism of evolutionary change, whereas the older point of view was chiefly concerned with sorting the results of evolution. . . . There has been almost no development of theory in physical anthropology itself, but the dominant attitude may be described as static, with emphasis on classification based on types."[73] Washburn's brief statement represented the culmination of decades of change in the biological sciences, which had finally effected a major paradigm shift in human evolutionary studies. He certainly agreed with Simpson that anthropologists were not generating evolutionary theory of their own, but predicted that emphasis would now be placed on evolution as a process rather than simply a pattern.

The "new" physical anthropology led to an understanding of our species' history more in line with current biological theory, and, somewhat ironically, was in some ways a return to evolutionary theory as expounded by Darwin nearly one hundred years earlier. Many of the evolutionary "laws" now being attacked by anthropologists were the same ones that Darwin himself would have rejected. According to Washburn, "Since Darwin's ideas could not be proved in detail by the techniques available in his time, the concept of selection did not become fully effective. Therefore, some pre-evolutionary ideas continued in full force. . . . For example, Lamarckian ideas have continued right down to today. Orthogenesis has been widely believed and irreversibility has been regarded as law."[74]

Finally, Washburn made one final plea to the anthropological community to shed its old theoretical baggage and fully accept the fundamental principles inherent in the evolutionary synthesis: "If a new physical anthropology is to differ effectively from the old, it must be more than the adoption of a little genetic terminology. It must change its ways of doing things to conform with the implications of modern evolutionary theory."[75]

The chair of the Cold Spring session, Harvard anthropologist W. W. Howells, was himself one of the new generation of physical anthropologists who recognized the changes occurring in the study of human evolution. He began his summation/commentary with a general statement: "The three preceding papers, though different in topic, agree strikingly in presenting a rejuvenated point of view on human-primate relationships. It has been in preparation for some years, with the finds of fossil material and the synthesis of genetic and paleontological thought, but in these three papers, written independently, it comes to a culmination."[76] As he had done in his text six years earlier, Howells again demonstrated his remarkable ability to recognize major changes as they were occurring. Aside from commenting on the "rejuvenated point of view" that humans and apes were indeed related phylogenetically, Howells argued that grade terminology had been responsible for a great deal of confusion in the past: "We have reached the point where some terms, especially 'human,' 'ape,' 'anthropoid' and 'man-ape,' are actually embarrassing, except as applied to living forms, or in the case of the last, to the South African australopiths. When we talk about anthropoid and human history, the word 'ape' keeps changing its meaning. . . . Although we cannot sweep them away by fiat, we should recognize that these terms, carried over from living animals, have their ambiguities. They do not represent well enough the actual quantities with which we are now dealing; these would be better represented by hominoid (for the whole group in all aspects), hominid (for the fruit of the bipedal adaptation), and pongid (for the arm-dependent apes, and their forerunners as well as we can distinguish them)."[77] For Howells, the use of grade terminology, which is necessarily subjective, had to be replaced with phylogenetic categories representing all of the members of a lineage rather than the living types. Howells also concurred with Washburn and Le Gros Clark that the adoption of habitual bipedalism was the first major adaptive change within the Hominidae, and that the question of classification was really a phyletic one: "It is now evident that the first hominids were small-brained, newly bipedal, proto-australopith hominoids, and that what we have always meant by 'man' represents later forms of this group with secondary adaptations in the direction of large brains and modified skeletons of the same form."[78]

Howells commented that a recent paper by Le Gros Clark was a fitting companion to the three from the session. Looking at that paper it is easy to see why Howells thought so: "The 'hominid sequence' must be taken to include all those intermediate forms which came into existence from the time when the divergence from the anthropoid sequence first took place. Clearly, therefore, the earliest members of the hominid sequence would still have shown many of the primitive features of the early anthropoid apes. . . . We no doubt tend in our minds to equate the term Hominidae with the large-brained members of the human family as we know it to-day, and to forget that the earlier representatives of the family, in the *aggregate* of their characters, must have approximated very closely to a simian level of evolutionary development."[79] Le Gros Clark's new inclusive approach to classification is evident in a phylogeny he published a few years later that clearly shows *Australopithecus* as an early, primitive stage of a larger hominid radiation (Fig 5.2).

With the adoption of the new evolutionary synthetic viewpoint,

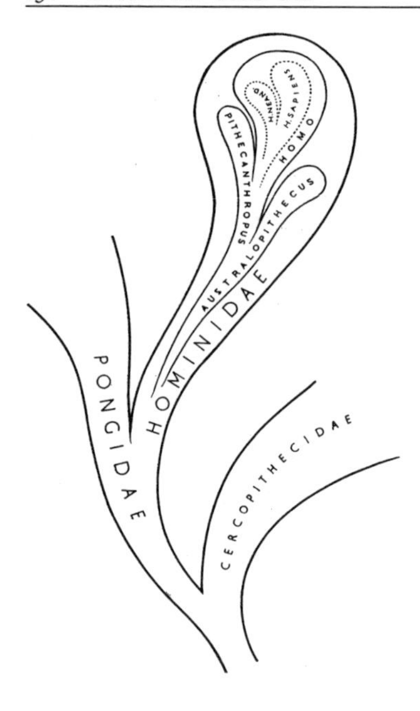

Fig. 5.2—Clark phylogeny (Clark 1955, p. 8).

classification became less of a preoccupation even as it became more straightforward: "As to classification, the australopiths go with man. It does not matter whether they are actually ancestral. . . . The main thing is a realistic relationship of all these animals on significant principles."[80] Howells also pointed out that previous attempts at reconstructing phylogeny had been oversimplified in that known fossil ape forms were assumed to be directly on the lineage leading to living ape forms. One of the outcomes of the synthesis was that a more appropriate metaphor for phylogeny was a tree with numerous branches, some ending in extinction, rather than a main trunk culminating with humans, with a few parallel lines leading toward the apes: "Let us look at the fossils first as indicators of the general process and scheme of development, until we have far more of them, instead of feeling obliged to put them into a given line at whatever effort, or use them as links in a chain already visualized."[81] In fact, if evolutionary theory had been in 1925 what it was when Howells was writing his remarks, the australopiths might have not only been embraced, but anticipated: "As Washburn says, after all the work on the comparative anatomy of the primates, no one thought to reconstruct a human ancestor possessing a human ilium and an ape's head. Yet, given present grasp of evolutionary theory in general, someone conceivably might have done this, before the finds of the australopiths showed such an actuality."[82]

The second session of the Cold Spring symposium, on fossil humans, was entitled "Classification of Fossil Men," and dealt mainly with the more recent stages of human evolution. In this session Harvard biologist Ernst Mayr gave one of the most influential papers in the history of paleoanthropology. He attempted to apply the same taxonomic criteria used by biologists studying organisms other than primates to humans and their extinct relatives. He began with the observation that "what in the case of *Drosophila* [the common fruit fly] is a genus has almost the rank of an order or, at least, suborder in the primates."[83] This taxonomic inflation was a result, according to Mayr, of the tendency of anthropologists to use a typological definition for species in which even the smallest differences were emphasized. But, he pointed out, "Anthropologists should never lose sight of the fact that taxonomic categories are based on populations, not on individuals."[84]

Mayr recommended, perhaps somewhat facetiously, that all of the known hominids, including the australopithecines, could be accommodated within one genus, *Homo*. Within this genus would be three species; *Homo sapiens, Homo erectus,* and, for the australopithecines, *Homo transvaalensis*. Dental and locomotor adaptations linked these species through time within the same lineage, despite other "minor" differences. As for why anthropologists had not come to a similar conclusion: "The principle objection [to an australopithecine ancestry for humans] that has been raised is that

South African man shows a combination of characters that 'should not' occur in an early hominid. This argument is based on typological considerations. Adherents of this concept believe that missing links should be about half-way between the forms they connect and that they should be half-way in every respect. This undoubtedly is not the case with *Australopithecus*. . . . The peculiar combination of characters that is found in *Australopithecus* is due to the fact that during the evolution of man different characters evolved at different rates."[85] Mayr firmly brought the australopithecines into the hominid family based on fundamental adaptations, even though other important hominid traits did not appear until later in the history of the lineage. His classification was based on morphology *and* phylogeny, not just the former.[86]

Despite the progress made at the Cold Spring Harbor symposium, it would take several more years before the australopithecines would be widely accepted as stem hominids, particularly outside of America, where most of the participants in the symposium had come from. In England, Le Gros Clark's series of papers on the australopithecines eventually led other Europeans to accept that the question of the phylogenetic placement of the South African species ultimately boiled down to the issue of bipedalism. By the end of the 1950s most publications dealing with human evolution included the australopithecines as primitive hominids, although only cautiously at times. Subsequent finds in eastern Africa that were firmly dated and the emergence of molecular anthropology ultimately put to rest any reservations.

Epilogue

> The adequate record of even the confusions of our forebears may help, not only to clarify those confusions, but to engender a salutary doubt whether we are wholly immune from different but equally great confusions.
>
> —ARTHUR LOVEJOY, *The Great Chain of Being*

In order to comprehend current scientific opinion on the origin of the human species, it is necessary to acquire firsthand knowledge of the historical development of such modern ideas. Documenting changing ideas, particularly regarding our own prehistory, is a fascinating exercise. The original words of Broom, Keith, Gregory, and Le Gros Clark, among many others, echo from the recent past about the more distant past. Not surprisingly, these scholars thought about human evolution in ways somewhat at odds with current ideas. Scientific research is by its nature an iterative process, and with each new discovery, theoretical breakthrough, or scholarly equivalent of the changing of the guard it is believed that a more accurate conclusion is reached.

The initial rejection of the australopithecines as human ancestors is typically explained with recourse to fairly specific reasons from within the field of anthropology having to do with dating, morphology, incomplete remains, and so forth. However, if the discussion is couched within the larger context of evolutionary biology, at least as anthropologists and anatomists practiced it, an additional factor is evident.

Prior to the adoption of the modern synthesis, anthropologists viewed evolutionary change as progressing along the predetermined temporalized Great Chain of Being. Orthogenesis was a convenient explanation for any humanlike anatomical traits of the South African fossils as the result of parallel evolution toward the same end. In retrospect this was clearly a case of "dressed up" teleology, with humans as the necessary goal of the evolutionary process.

For a few prescient individuals, the features that the australopithecines shared with *Homo sapiens* were evidence of shared ancestry. This only became clear to a majority of scholars during the late 1940s, when orthogenesis was being challenged as a legitimate evolutionary force. While parallelism may have been considered adequate to explain away cranio-dental similarities, the obvious humanlike details of the australopithecine pelvis as it related to bipedal locomotion were much more difficult to dismiss. This new perspective came about when paleoanthropologists adopted a view of evolution more in line with that of biologists, paleontologists, and geneticists.[1] If a single moment in time when such a transformation occurred can be identified, it was the convening of the Cold Spring Harbor symposium of 1950 on the evolution of humans.

The modern synthesis was by that time disseminated throughout the biological community in the wide sense, but had not really had a significant impact on anthropology. By the conclusion of the conference, however, it was clear that attention was now focused on evolving populations rather than individual types. The disjunction between phylogeny and gradistic classification had crumbled, and it was now apparent that the South African "man-apes" were on the line of ancestry leading to modern humans. Hence they were classified as primitive members of the Hominidae, despite their grade status as apes. After the publication of the proceedings the following year, the stage was set for the dismissal of the old approach to paleoanthropology and the induction of the "new" physical anthropology.

The Last Fifty Years

The results of scientific research over the intervening decades since the Cold Spring symposium have been consistent with the now seemingly incontrovertible fact that modern human beings are descended from African apes. While there is some debate about how the modern synthesis has shaped subsequent hominid evolutionary analyses in general,[2] it cannot be denied that on balance the application of neo-Darwinian principles to questions of human ancestry was a positive, if not final, step.

The 1950s can be viewed as a period of fundamental change for human evolutionary studies. For one thing, several of the key players involved in the original australopithecine debate passed away. Broom died in 1951, only days after completing his last monograph (Broom and Robinson 1952). Broom's understudy John Robinson emerged as an instrumental leader in the effort to enforce the place of the australopithecines within human phylogeny, but with a much more contemporary view of evolution than that held by Broom. He published a series of papers in which he attempted to put the australopithecines in an adaptive light based on the influence of the synthesis, rather than obsessing on taxonomic details. Although the result was a lumping of many of Broom's species into a smaller number of taxa, Robinson proposed that the South African australopithecines were nonetheless a diverse group, not heeding Mayr's suggestion of a single hominid genus. Specifically, he viewed *Paranthropus* and *Australopithecus* as occupying separate ecological niches based on their diets (Robinson 1954; compare with Broom 1950b).

Sir Arthur Keith passed away in 1955 and fellow English anatomist W. L. H. Duckworth passed away in 1956, leaving British physical anthropology in the hands of a new generation of scholars, such as Le Gros Clark, Louis Leakey, and Michael Day. In the United States, Harvard anthropologist E. A. Hooton died in 1954, Yale's R. S.

Lull in 1957, and Franz Weidenreich, then of the American Museum of Natural History, passed away in 1948. The void in the United States was filled in by William Howells at Wisconsin (later Harvard) and Sherwood Washburn at Chicago (later Berkeley), among others.

The Piltdown fossils were exposed as a deliberate fraud in 1953,[3] and while the effect that "*Eoanthropus*" had on the interpretation of the australopithecines outside of England is debatable, the elimination of this form, which was at odds with virtually every other fossil human, probably helped nonetheless to solidify the australopithecines' place on the human family tree.

Still, the australopithecines were not completely embraced with open arms. For example, in the 1952 edition of the French text *Fossil Men*, the new view of the australopithecines was apparent, but some reservation remained. Bipedalism was now considered an important trait in establishing phylogeny, but as for the classification of these fossils, author Henri Vallois presented three alternatives:

> They are true anthropoids, allied to the Gorilla and Chimpanzee, although possessing certain features curiously reminiscent of Man. . . . At the opposite extreme, Dart and later Broom and Le Gros Clark, declare categorically that the Australopithecinae are already Hominids, their resemblances to Man being far too numerous to be explained otherwise than by a direct relationship. . . . The majority of palaeontologists subscribe to a theory that is, in a sense, intermediate between the two foregoing. According to this view, the Australopithecinae are a group of Anthropoids in the process of evolving towards humanity, but which never crossed the "threshold" to this condition and vanished without having become truly human. . . . Human as they are in their dentition and posture, the Australopithecinae are none the less Apes in terms of their brain. . . . Far from being our ancestors, these Primates may only have been, in the phrase of Gregory and Hellman, "Man's less evolved cousins."[4]

In this case, the failure to make a distinction between human and hominid continued to confuse the issue. As the large brain was still considered the paramount human feature, the South African fossils could not be called human. If they were not human, they were not hominid, and therefore not ancestral.

Louis Leakey completely rewrote his general human evolutionary text, *Adam's Ancestors,* in 1953, and was somewhat ambivalent about the significance of the australopithecines. He had visited South Africa in 1949 and studied the original fossils, after which he sent off a note to Ralph von Koenigswald: "I am convinced that they were (a) very close to the stock from which man came, (b) much too late in geological time (they are Pleistocene) to be ancestral to man, (c) are far too specialised in certain unexpected ways . . . to be regarded as representing even a Pleistocene survival of the type of creature from which man evolved. In my opinion they represent an offshoot from the stock from which man arose."[5] He certainly did not view them with the same enthusiasm as Le Gros Clark, Howells, Dart, Washburn, and the like. Leakey continued to wrestle with grade versus clade classification: "This combination of characters has led some scientists to conclude that the South African Australopithecinae should be classified at the extreme lower limit of the hominidae, and just within the range of man."[6] He was still making the mistake of equating Hominidae and human, which naturally led him to question the conclusion that the australopithecines, while not being human, could still be ranked among the hominids: "The terms 'man' and 'human' have come to have a definite significance for most of us, and among other things they suggest: (1) a brain size larger than that found in any of the South African 'near-men'; (2) a tool-making creature."[7] Leakey did not uncritically accept Broom's inflated cranial capacity for *Paranthropus crassidens,* or Dart's osteodontokeratic culture. Although time has shown that he was correct in his criticism on both counts, it is clear that he was still demanding a certain level, or grade, of development in defining humans, but also in defining the Hominidae. Regardless of his reservations, the phylogeny published in the new edition of his book showed the australopithecines as a low branch off of the main hominid lineage. This style was very typical in that it allowed the australopithecines to be related to humans without being in their direct line.

Von Koenigswald also was conflicted over the significance of the South African species, no doubt partly due to his interest in maintaining the Java fossils he had helped discover as the oldest and most primitive hominids. Despite the humanlike traits of the australopithecines he resurrected the overspecialization/irreversibility argument to remove them from human ancestry: "So many features which must be regarded as a sign of over-specialization . . . exclude the Australopithecinae from the ancestorship not only of *Pithecanthropus* but also of *Homo sapiens*." Although he did not view them as direct human ancestors, he nonetheless stated unambiguously that the fossils did represent primitive members of the human family, which probably went extinct without issue: "The Australopithecinae apparently are a group of the Hominidae, which most probably did not rise much above the 'anthropoid' level."[8] Von Koenigswald had grasped the essential point that the family Hominidae contained apes as well as later humans. They did sit on a branch of the hominid family tree, albeit occupying a spot near the pongid-hominid split: "The discovery of the australopiths has given an entirely new slant to the problem of the coming of man. Previously people believed in an antithesis, Man-Ape, and supposed that man must inescapably fulfill his human destiny. Now this has been proved an illusion. Only one branch of the Hominids—perhaps with a few secondary offshoots—bit into the apple of knowledge and reached the summit from which their eyes could gaze not only into their immediate surroundings but into the cosmos. Another, conservative branch was unable to free itself from its attachment to its animal origins. *Australopithecus* is a tragic case: he was left behind in the school of life. It would be a mistake to blame this on his teacher."[9] This is very similar to Leakey's position, and what is noteworthy is that no matter how much the australopithecines were viewed as primitive, they were nonetheless included as part of the hominid radiation. This sort of thought process, which considered populations and evolving lineages rather than simple types, was a direct outcome of the diffusion of the modern synthesis into paleoanthropology.

By the early 1960s, the last serious attempts to exclude the australopithecines from the Hominidae had come and gone (Ashton and Zuckerman 1950, for example), partly because one of the main impediments had been removed. Although the *relative* ages of fossil hominid species were fairly well established, estimates of absolute (numerical) age were quite varied. Even so, no scientist had suspected the great antiquity that was demonstrated by the first radiometric dates obtained from lavas collected at Olduvai Gorge in northern Tanzania. Louis and Mary Leakey had been working at Olduvai since the 1930s, and although they had collected many stone tools and nonhominid faunal remains, they had not been able to recover any significant hominid fossils. Their luck changed in 1959 when Mary discovered the cranium of a "hyper" robust australopithecine that they later referred to the novel genus *Zinjanthropus* (Leakey 1959). A year later the new potassium-argon dating technique (K/Ar) was applied at Olduvai and provided an astonishing date of about 1.75 million years ago (mya), essentially double what was expected (Leakey et al. 1961). This new evidence for the deep antiquity of the earliest known hominids effectively eliminated the argument that the australopithecines were too young geologically speaking to be direct human ancestors. This was especially important for the Leakeys at Olduvai, as *Zinjanthropus* was found in association with stone tools, a universally accepted human hallmark, doubly confirming the hominid status of their australopithecine.[10]

The introduction of these new absolute dates and the belief that more primitive hominids were waiting to be found resulted in claims for even older ancestors. Historically, many scholars (such as Sir Arthur Keith) had believed that the *Homo sapiens* lineage might extend into the Miocene epoch—of course they could not have known that this geological period extended from 5 to nearly 25 mya. Hence, despite the surprisingly old dates for the basal Pleistocene at Olduvai, field researchers looked to the Pliocene and Miocene for even older hominids. In the early 1960s, Elwyn Simons of Yale University resurrected the idea that the Siwalik species *Ramapithecus*, known only from teeth and jaws, was an early hominid (Simons 1961). G. E. Lewis had suggested the same thing back in the 1930s, but the idea was soundly rejected by Hrdlicka, among others. In addition, Louis Leakey proposed *Kenyapithecus wickeri* from Fort Ternan as an early hominid (Leakey 1962). Both of these fossils were of Miocene age, and their consideration as hominids reflected the widely accepted notion that the human lineage was a deep one, perhaps diverging from the apes as far back as 20 mya.

A second major development during the 1960s was the reintroduction of molecular studies into the classification of the higher primates. While the radiometric dates had the effect of greatly increasing the time span of hominid evolution, comparative blood protein research had the opposite effect of constraining how old a hominid could be, thereby challenging the assumption that human ancestors had existed in the Miocene. Nuttall (1904) is often cited as a pioneer of using molecular studies to infer relationships among the primates, but it was not until the early 1960s, when Nuttall's analysis was revisited by Morris Goodman of Wayne State University, that it was proved once and for all that the African apes were our closest relatives, and that counterarguments were no longer tenable at a morphological or a molecular level (Goodman 1963). The question of the timing of the divergence of the African apes and the Hominidae remained unresolved, however.

In 1967 Berkeley scientists Vince Sarich and Alan Wilson addressed the question of timing, and superimposed an absolute time scale onto the relationships established by Goodman. Using their concept of a molecular clock, which suggested that DNA mutations accumulated at a roughly constant rate, they concluded that hominids had diverged from the African apes sometime around 4 to 5 mya (Sarich and Wilson 1967). Significantly, they calibrated the clock using a fairly well established divergence point based on the fossil record. Therefore, as Sarich so bluntly stated, any fossil older than this time range could not be a hominid, no matter what it looked like. The best candidate for the earliest hominid at the time, *Ramapithecus* (including *Kenyapithecus* from Fort Ternan in some classification systems), was dated to the middle Miocene and therefore outside of the molecular time range, which meant that it could not be a hominid. The morphologists were outraged by Sarich's bold statement, but time, and the fossil record, have supported his once contentious position.[11]

The late 1960s also yielded a significant development in field research methodology. Paleoanthropologists adopted a new multidisciplinary approach to fieldwork that placed the recovered hominid fossils in a firm chronometric and paleoenvironmental context. If early hominids were to be viewed as individual members of evolving populations adapting to specific local environments, it became necessary to reconstruct these ancient habitats, as well as the human ancestors themselves. Hence, paleoanthropology became a specialized field requiring the input of scientists with many different backgrounds. A multinational research effort carried out along the Omo River valley of southern Ethiopia was the first major project to follow this new approach (Coppens et al. 1976). Only a few fragmentary hominid specimens were collected, but further north in Ethiopia, at the site of Hadar, numerous australopithecines were recovered beginning in the early 1970s that appeared to be even more anatomically primitive and more geologically ancient than those already known. As a result, the first new hominid species in fifteen years was named for the Hadar hominids (Johanson et al. 1978), and similar fossils collected at Laetoli in northern Tanzania by Mary Leakey's team.[12] Soon after the announcement of *Australopithecus afarensis,* a view of hominid evolution emerged that placed this new species at the root of the family tree, from which later australopithecines evolved, followed by three successive species of *Homo* (Johanson and White 1979).

Current Views of the Hominidae

Paleoanthropologists are unified in their understanding of the broad facts surrounding early human evolution. Based on genetic and morphological analyses, the African apes are indisputably our nearest living relatives. Using the molecular clock as a rough guide and judging from the known fossil record, it can be stated with some certainty that the human lineage diverged from the African ape lineage sometime around 5 to 7 mya. Soon after this split, hominids began to diversify throughout Africa. This general consensus notwithstanding, higher-resolution molecular studies, competing systematic philosophies, and especially new fossil finds continue to provide fodder for debate surrounding the early evolution of the Hominidae.

The last decade has witnessed a dramatic increase in the number of early hominid fossil discoveries (White et al. 1994, 1995; Leakey et al. 1994; Brunet et al. 1996; Clarke 1998; Haile-Selassie 2001; Senut et al. 2001; Brunet et al. 2002), suggesting that the base of the human family tree may be more complex than previously thought. Consequently, in describing early hominid phylogeny some anthropologists have abandoned the tree metaphor in favor of a bush (Lieberman 2001, Wood 2002). It is argued that this diverse evolutionary pattern is completely in keeping with those of other medium- to large-bodied African mammalian lineages, such as pigs, monkeys, and horses.[13]

These recent discoveries remind us that any given definition for the Hominidae is likely to be revised as these fossils show unexpected mosaics of hominid and African ape features. For example, initial indications suggest that *Ardipithecus ramidus ramidus*, a 4.4 million-year-old species from Ethiopia, is bipedal, yet exhibits other morphological features, such as thin tooth enamel and primitive deciduous third premolars, that are associated with modern chimpanzees and gorillas (White et al. 1994, 1995).

This new evidence also calls into question our ability to recognize the very earliest members of the hominid lineage. Since bipedalism is *the* trait that distinguishes the Hominidae as traditionally defined, we may reasonably ask whether bipedalism is being treated the same way that large brain size was in the past. In other words, if bipedalism is the new threshold for inclusion in the Hominidae, is a situation created in which we may be unable to detect the earliest members of our lineage in the fossil record? If the human lineage diverged from the African ape lineage *before* the evolution of bipedalism, this is a distinct possibility.

We may also ruminate on the possibility that if bipedalism conferred some significant adaptive advantage to early hominids, as virtually all paleoanthropologists believe,[14] it may have evolved in other nonhominid African ape lineages that left no descendants. While arguments for evolution being goal-oriented are no longer seriously considered, there has been some discussion of canalization within lineages due to the limitations imposed by ancestry. If the resultant parallel evolution (homoplasy) is as common as some paleontologists suspect, it might be possible that the evidence for bipedalism found in some of the oldest and most primitive fossils is not due to common ancestry. A reanalysis of the postcranial skeleton of *Oreopithecus*, a Miocene ape from Italy, seems to show convergent features with *Australopithecus* linked to bipedalism (Kohler and Moya-Sola 1997). Recently collected associated cranial and postcranial remains from Sterkfontein display a combination of features significantly different from roughly contemporaneous *A. afarensis* fossils (Berger 2002).[15] Could there have been more than one bipedal lineage extant during the early Pliocene?

A final paleontological concern has to do with the known hominid fossil record as it currently stands. Hominid remains can only be collected where fossiliferous sedimentary deposits of the right age are exposed. As a result we have recovered fossils from only a very small part of the African continent. In some basic way this has to affect the probability that we have sampled a population directly ancestral to modern humans. Fossils from Chad are expanding the known geographic range of early australopithecines, and it is somewhat reassuring that one specimen, the anterior part of a mandible with several teeth, looks similar to contemporaneous *A. afarensis* from eastern Africa (Brunet et al. 1995, 1996).[16] It is possible and even likely that the discovery of additional late Miocene and early Pliocene hominids in other parts of Africa will demonstrate greater variation than is currently known, and may reveal further surprises in terms of defining the morphology of the earliest Hominidae.[17]

In addition to the increase in early hominid fossil material, DNA analyses have continued to influence the debate about our earliest ancestors in unprecedented ways. Decades ago molecular studies of living hominoids effectively constrained the age of the earliest hominids, eventually to most paleontologists' satisfaction. More recently, higher-resolution methods purporting to resolve the African ape and human "trichotomy" remain at least mildly contentious. A majority of these studies suggest that chimpanzees and humans share a common ancestor to the exclusion of the gorilla (Ruvolo 1997). If this is accurate, it has obvious implications for our reconstruction of the earliest hominids, not least of which is that they may have been direct descendants of knuckle-walkers (Richmond et al. 2001).

The now widely accepted conclusion that a *Pan-Homo* clade is a reality reflects a broader trend in which genetic analyses, particularly those that have directly sequenced DNA at various well-studied loci, are perceived as more reliable than more traditional morphological or even molecular analyses. This perception has led at least some scientists to seriously question the ability of hard tissues in particular to resolve phylogenetic relationships (Collard and Wood 2000). This essentially is a continuation of what Sarich and Wilson began almost forty years ago when they first challenged the utility of the fossil record in identifying actual phylogenetic relationships.

While the total data bearing on human phylogeny have grown and diversified, there is no reason to suspect that we have discovered the definitive branching sequence for our lineage. On the one hand, we accept human evolution as historical fact, and recognize that there can be only one right answer in terms of phylogeny. We would like to believe, of course, that we move incrementally closer to "the truth" with each fossil discovery, analytical breakthrough, generation of anthropologists, etc. This study has shown that the data at our disposal, and, more broadly, the scientific and social contexts within which we work naturally influence our conclusions. Paleoanthropologists need to be cognizant of this fact, and also need to maintain a historical perspective that allows us to review what has been done previously and justify why our new conclusions are more justifiable. If nothing else, careful study of paleoanthropological history reminds us to remain critical of what we think we currently know about the earliest phases of our evolutionary past.

Appendixes

A.1: Humanlike Traits of the Taung Fossil Originally Noted by Dart in 1925.

1. Vertically implanted incisors.
2. Greatly reduced size of the canine tooth, coupled with the absence of a mandibular diastema, and only a small maxillary diastema.
3. Morphology of the milk molars, especially nonsectorial dm_1.
4. Forward placement of the foramen magnum (suggesting erect posture).
5. Vertical frontal squama.
6. Lack of apelike brow ridges.
7. Humanlike position of the inferior border of the nasal bones relative to eye orbits.
8. Increased separation of the lunate and parallel sulci on the brain endocast.

A.2: Criticisms Leveled Against Dart's Interpretation.

1. Humanlike features were due to parallelism.
2. Humanlike features were due to the young biological age of the individual.
3. The Taung fossil was geologically too young to be ancestral to humans.
4. The evidence for bipedalism was inadequate without postcranial remains.
5. Overall brain size was outside the range for humans.
6. Southern Africa was not a likely "cradle of humankind"; Asia was more likely.
7. Dart had no comparative sample, especially of young chimpanzees.
8. Dart was too hasty (taking less than three months from discovery to publication).

A.3: Major Australopithecine Fossils Collected Between 1936 and 1946

Specimen	Taxon	Published
Partial cranium (S1); R and L maxillae P^3-M^3/endocast	Plesianthropus*	1936
Isolated right M_3	Plesianthropus	1937
Isolated M^3, I^1, worn M3	Plesianthropus	1938
Female right maxilla (S2); I^2-C^1-P^3-M^1	Plesianthropus†	1938
Isolated female? C_1	Plesianthropus	1938
Juvenile male anterior mandible w/left C_1	Plesianthropus	1938
Isolated left P_4	Plesia nthropus	1938
Partial skull, P2-M3	Paranthropus‡	1938
Old male left maxilla; cast of skullcap (S3)	Plesianthropus	1938
Distal left femur	Plesianthropus	1938
Distal right humerus/proximal right ulna; distal pedal phalanx (2nd?)	Paranthropus	1938
Left M^3§	Plesianthropus ?	1939
Capitate (Os magnum)	Plesianthropus	1941
Juvenile mandible w/i^2, c^1, $dm^{1,2}$	Paranthropus	1941
2nd metacarpal and proximal phalanx; proximal manual phalanx (4th?)	Paranthropus	1942
Right talus	Paranthropus	1943

*Type of *Plesianthropus transvaalensis* (originally described as *Australopithecus transvaalensis*).

†The female maxilla was considered by Broom as the "topotype."

‡Type of *Paranthropus robustus*. All *Paranthropus* specimens are from Kromdraai.

§All *Plesianthropus* specimens are from Sterkfontein except this left third molar (upper), which was collected at Cooper's Farm.

A.4: Major Australopithecine Fossils Collected Between 1947 and 1950

Specimen	Taxon	Published
Two fragmentary maxillae (infant and subadult)	Plesianthropus*	1947
Isolated male C^1, mandibular molar	Plesianthropus	1947
Nearly complete endentulous cranium	Plesianthropus	1947
Male mandible, fragmetary maxilla, proximal humerus, fragmentary scapula	Plesianthropus	1947
Fragmentary skeleton; includes innominate, proximal humerus, fragmentary femur and tibia, vertebrae, cranial fragments	Plesianthropus	1947
Partial cranium (no. 8)	Plesianthropus	1948
Male mandible w/I_1-M_3	Plesianthropus	1948
Occipital	Australopithecus†	1948
Juvenile mandible	Australopithecus	1948
Partial face, maxilla w/P^3-M^2	Australopithecus	1948
Adolescent pelvis	Australopithecus	1948
Distal femur	Plesianthropus	1949
Male mandible w/C_1-M_3	Plesianthropus	1949
Mandible w/P_2-M_3	Paranthropus‡	1949
Maxillary fragment w/I^1, I^2, C^1	Paranthropus	1949
Crushed calotte and fragmentary female maxilla w/P3–4, M^1	Paranthropus	1949/1950
Mandible w/P_3-M_3, fragmentary maxilla and lower face	Paranthropus	1949
Crushed juvenile cranium	Paranthropus	1949
Right first metacarpal	Paranthropus	1949
Two partial crania (nos. 6, 7)	Plesianthropus	1950
Juvenile mandible w/dm1–2, c, I_1	Paranthropus	1950
Female mandible w/complete dentition	Paranthropus	1950
Partial innominate	Paranthropus	1950
Female cranium	Paranthropus	1950

*All *Plesianthropus* specimens are from Sterkfontein.

†Type of *Australopithecus prometheus*. All specimens from Makapansgat.

‡Type of *Paranthropus crassidens*. All specimens are from Swartkrans.

Notes

Prologue

1. This is the biological group (clade) to which humans and their extinct ancestors belong. For many current scholars this group is distinguished at some lower taxonomic level, these days usually the tribe Hominini. In this study I maintain the traditional use of Hominidae simply to be consistent with the historical literature. For the same reason I use the subfamily designation Australopithecinae for all of the African "bipedal apes." This group is certainly paraphyletic, to use the modern jargon, and as a result an increasing number of scholars prefer to use the less formal term australopith to lump together the various African species.
2. Darwin 1871, p. 520.
3. Ibid.

Chapter 1. The Great Chain Legacy

1. Lovejoy 1936, p. 242.
2. Three sources—Yerkes and Yerkes 1929; McDermott 1938; and Janson 1952—were used extensively for this survey, along with a host of primary and other secondary sources where indicated.
3. Lovejoy's classic work summarizing the history of the Chain of Being is the main source of information on this topic in this chapter. In the title to his work Lovejoy added the word "Great" to the Chain of Being; throughout this book I use these terms interchangeably.
4. This is also one of the reasons why extinction was later viewed as such a threat.
5. Aristotle, quoted in Thijssen 1995, p. 44.

6. Herodotus c. 440 B.C., book IV, chapter 191.

7. Pliny c. 77 A.D., book VII, para. 21, 23.

8. Ibid., book V, para. 46.

9. Wittkower 1942, pp. 165–166.

10. Here I use the terms monkey and ape in their modern taxonomic sense (i.e., superfamily Cercopithecoidea vs. Hominoidea).

11. Quoted in Yerkes and Yerkes 1929, p. 3.

12. McDermott (1938) indicates that in a few cases it appears that ancient writers provided reliable accounts of true anthropoid apes. However, these are written accounts, and in no case is a definite pictorial likeness of any anthropoid ape species given.

13. Aristotle fourth century B.C., book 2, chapters 8, 9. The fact that Aristotle says the baboon is larger than the ape supports the argument that the ape referred to was the Barbary macaque, which possesses only a rudimentary tail.

14. Pliny c. 77 A.D., book VII, para. 24.

15. Ibid., book VIII, para. 215.

16. Galen c. 192 A.D., book I, chapter 2.

17. Ibid. Yerkes and Yerkes (1929) suggest that Galen may have actually dissected an orangutan, since he mentioned the laryngeal bladders later described by Camper in the eighteenth century. However, laryngeal sacs are variably expressed in a number of other primates, including some Old World monkeys.

18. St. Augustine c. 427 A.D., book 6, chapter 16.

19. Ibid., book 16, chapter 8. Note that the translator's choice of the chimpanzee is not to be uncritically accepted.

20. Battell 1624, p. 54.

21. Tyson 1699.

22. Ibid., p. 5.

23. Buffon 1766.

24. Ibid.

25. Ibid.

26. The first definite account of the lowland gorilla doesn't occur until 1847 (incidentally, as "a new species of Orang"), and the mountain gorilla was first described in 1903. The pygmy chimpanzee, or bonobo, was not described as a distinct animal until 1929.

27. Camper 1779, pp. 145–147, 153.

28. Linnaeus 1746, quoted in Bendysche 1864, pp. 444–445.

29. Emmanuel Hoppius, a student of Linnaeus, figured some of Linnaeus's primate species in 1760. Clearly seen is the chimpanzee, here called *Simia satyrus*, and what is probably a gibbon. Linnaeus's wild man, or *Troglodytes* in the figure, is human.

30. Linnaeus 1759, quoted in Bendysche 1864, pp. 435–437.

Chapter 2. Putting the Chain in Motion

1. Hutton 1794.

2. Stone tools had been collected for some time before they were finally accepted in the early eighteenth century as bona fide cultural remains of prehistoric people. They were initially considered to be nothing more than interesting geological features. Later it was surmised that early humans utilized stone to manufacture implements before the use of metals was developed. In the early 1800s Danish archeologists formalized these periods into the Stone, Bronze, and Iron Ages, and in 1865 John Lubbock further divided the Stone Age into the Paleolithic and Neolithic in his influential text *Prehistoric Times.*

3. Frere's letter was written in 1797 and published in 1800. The quote is taken from the letter as reprinted in Grayson 1983.

4. At the turn of the century people were just coming to accept that extinction was possible, mainly through the comparative anatomy research of French paleontologist Georges Cuvier. The idea that humans could have shared the landscape with these "failures" was rejected.

5. See Grayson 1983 for a full discussion of the coincidental, but not causal, acceptance of the ancientness of humans and of organic evolution in 1859 and the years that followed.

6. Foucault 1970, p. 125.

7. Darwin 1794, pp. 552–553.

8. See Burkhardt 1995 for a thorough discussion of Lamarck's evolutionary biology.

9. Lamarck 1809, p. 170.

10. Ibid., p. 58.

11. Lovejoy 1936, p. 255.

12. This idea that humans had a very deep evolutionary past remained pervasive throughout the first decades of the twentieth century; it was later formalized into the "Pre-sapiens" model of human origins.

13. Morse 1884, p. 12.

14. Mivart 1874, pp. 4–5, 193.

15. Darwin 1871, pp. 398, 519.

16. Huxley 1863, pp. 97, 143–144.

17. Hartmann 1886, pp. 287–288.

18. Wallace 1889, pp. 307, 308.

19. Ibid., p. 308.

20. Garner 1900, pp. 2, 85, 211.

21. Darwin 1859, pp. 373–374.

22. Ibid., p. 373.

23. Darwin 1871, pp. 433–436.

24. Ibid., p. 520.

25. Cartmill 2001, p. 99.

Chapter 3. Finding Missing Links

1. The term ape was often used to describe any anthropoid primate; for example, Mivart discussed "the American Apes" in reference to New World monkeys, and Hartmann referred to the Hanuman Langur as the slender ape. Here I am using the term ape in the modern sense: nonhominid members of the Hominoidea.

2. Placing higher primate fossils, even those of great antiquity, on a direct ancestral branch leading to living species remained very common up until the 1970s (see, for example, Simons and Pilbeam's revision of the Hominoidea in 1965).

3. Now Pakistan.

4. There is some debate over whether the discovery and description of this tooth preceded the report by Lartet (see Kennedy and Ciochon 1999).

5. *Troglodytes* was the genus originally used for the chimpanzee, and later the gorilla when the latter was described as a distinct species in 1847. By 1896 *Troglodytes* was still retained for the chimpanzee, but the gorilla was given its own genus, *Gorilla*. Later on, a new genus, *Pan,* was created for the chimpanzee, although *troglodytes* was retained as the trivial name.

6. Lydekker 1896, p. 3.

7. In fairness to the original discoverers, juveniles are notoriously difficult to distinguish among closely related species relative to adult specimens. This is, ironically, one of the reasons why *Australopithecus,* the subject of Chapters 4 and 5, was greeted with skepticism by many anthropologists in 1925.

8. Beginning in 1997 more of this original skeleton, along with fauna and stone artifacts, was recovered within sediments removed from the cave in 1856 (Schmitz et al. 2002).

9. Schaaffhausen 1861, p. 172.

10. Huxley 1864, p. 443.

11. Hartmann 1886, pp. 115–116.

12. Quoted in Gruber 1948. Although Falconer seemed to be suggesting that this fossil represented *Homo sapiens,* albeit a primitive type, he curiously decided with Busk's permission to name it *Homo calpicus,* after the ancient name for Gibraltar. This informal usage of a new species name begs the question of what, if any, species concept existed at the time.

13. Detailed explications of the early Neandertal discoveries can be found in Stringer and Gamble 1993; Trinkaus and Shipman 1992; and Bowler 1986.

14. For a detailed exposition on Dubois and *Pithecanthropus,* see Shipman 2001.

15. This specimen, and a second collected by Dubois himself, are now considered to belong to *Homo sapiens*.

16. Fossils originally attributed to *Pithecanthropus* are now included in the species *Homo erectus*.

17. Dubois 1898, p. 449.

18. Cunningham 1895a, p. 428.

19. Dubois 1896, pp. 246–247.

20. This specimen was later given a separate genus name, *Palaeanthropus*. Currently the fossil is allocated to a loosely defined group of hominids called "archaic" *H. sapiens*, or is considered the type specimen of *Homo heidelbergensis*, a species that may have evolved into the Neandertals in Europe.

21. McCabe 1910, pp. 18–19.

22. The assumption that the evolution of a large brain occurred prior to other changes undoubtedly influenced the interpretation of *Australopithecus* (e.g., Hammond 1988; Spencer 1990). Had scientists been secure in the idea that bipedalism came first, the South African fossils would have provided welcome support. However, as the following chapters will demonstrate, despite evidence beginning with Taung that suggested a bipedal gait for the australopithecines, discussion revolved much more around the teeth and cranial anatomy of the fossils, and locomotor pattern was infrequently discussed.

23. Osborn 1927, p. 47.

24. Gregory 1914, p. 190. While Gregory may not have actually believed this himself, he was nonetheless very cautious when writing about Piltdown.

25. Lydekker 1915, p. 277.

26. Gregory 1915, p. 342.

27. Gregory 1916, p. 293.

28. Smith 1924.

29. Keith, unpublished manuscript, "The Line of Human Descent," pp. 4–5, Keith Collection, Box XAC, Royal College of Surgeons, London.

Chapter 4. The Southern Ape

1. Howells 1951, p. 80.

2. There were a few dissenting opinions, most notably on the part of H. F. Osborn in the United States and F. Wood Jones in England, who, for different reasons, rejected an ape ancestry for humans.

3. Reviews of Dart's early years, along with details of the initial discovery of the Taung fossil, can be found in Wheelhouse and Smithford 2001, Tobias 1984, Wheelhouse 1983, and Dart and Craig 1959.

4. In a letter to Arthur Keith a few months later, Dart wrote, "The specimen came to me on Nov 28th and my paper went away on Jan. 6th so you will judge that many things remain to be done." Letter dated 26 Feb. 1925, Keith Collection, Box KL1, Envelope D, Royal College of Surgeons, London.

5. A South African periodical, *The Star*, published a short article on the Taung fossil on Feb. 3, and the London Times announced the find on Feb. 4 and 6.

6. Dart 1925a, p. 198.

7. Ibid., p. 195.

8. This family designation was never accepted, and in later publications, despite his belief that *Australopithecus* did have a place on the human family tree, Dart referred to the fossil as a member of the Australopithecidae.

9. Smith 1925a, p. 235.

10. Ibid.

11. Smith 1925b, p. 240.

12. Now Zambia.

13. Woodward 1925, pp. 235–236.

14. Journal entry, Jan. 1925, Keith Collection, Box D1.

15. Keith 1925b, p. 234.

16. Dart 1925a, p. 197.

17. Keith 1925c, p. 326.

18. Letter dated 26 Feb. 1925, Keith Collection, Box KL1, Envelope D.

19. In early publications the town of Taung, as it is now known, was commonly referred to as Taungs.

20. Elliot Smith Lecture, May 1925, quoted from the *London Times* in Broom and Schepers 1946, p. 16.

21. Journal entry, 20 June 1925, Keith Collection, Box D1, Diary and Summary 1921–1932.

22. Keith 1925d, p. 11.

23. Broom 1925a, p. 571.

24. Ibid., p. 570.

25. Keith 1925d, p. 11.

26. Broom 1925b, p. 414.

27. Letter from Sollas to Broom, 24 Mar. 1925, quoted in Broom 1950a, p. 25.

28. Sollas 1925, p. 909.

29. Letter from Sollas to Broom, 25 May 1925, quoted in Broom 1950a, p. 26.

30. Letter from Sollas to Broom, quoted in Findlay 1972, p. 53.

31. Letter from Dubois to Keith, 2 Apr. 1925, Keith Collection, Box KL1, Envelope D.

32. Howells 1985, pp. 20–24.

33. Hooton 1927, p. 141.

34. Hooton 1931, p. 381.

35. Ibid., p. 390.

36. Hrdlicka's family emigrated to New York in 1882. In 1903 he was appointed assistant curator at the National Museum (Smithsonian); he was appointed full curator in charge of physical anthropology in 1910.

37. Hrdlicka 1925, pp. 390–392.

38. Unpublished manuscript, Hrdlicka Collection, National Anthropological Archives, Washington, D.C.

39. Unpublished letter from Hrdlicka to Dubois, 26 Oct. 1925, Hrdlicka Collection.

40. Unpublished letter from Hrdlicka to Elliot Smith, 3 Nov. 1925, Hrdlicka Collection.

41. It may be telling that Hrdlicka sent complimentary copies of his 1930 compendium, *The Skeletal Remains of Early Man,* to several colleagues in London—including Keith, and also Black, Boule, and Dubois—but not to Dart or Broom.

42. Miller 1928, p. 415.

43. Ibid., p. 422.

44. Ibid.

45. Ibid., pp. 415–416.

46. It is tempting to surmise that Miller's opinion may reflect Hrdlicka's influence, since they were both at the Smithsonian Institution.

47. Wilder 1926, pp. 78–79.

48. Ibid., p. 25 (fn).

49. Ibid., p. 138.

50. Ibid., pp. 219–220.

51. Between 1926 and 1930, Gregory and Osborn wrote numerous articles on the subject of early human ancestry, often publishing simultaneously in the same journal. Although these were cordial, it was quite clear that Gregory thought Osborn was on very shaky ground, and one wonders if Gregory would have been so gracious had Osborn not been his boss at the museum.

52. Gregory 1927, p. 555.

53. Letter from Gregory to Dart, 24 Jan. 1930, Gregory Collection no. 1, Box 5, American Museum of Natural History, New York.

54. Letter from Gregory to Dart, 3 May 1930, Gregory Collection no. 1, Box 5.

55. Gregory 1930a, p. 160.

56. Letter from Hrdlicka to Gregory, 25 Apr. 1930, Hrdlicka Collection.

57. Gregory 1930b, p. 650.

58. Unpublished phylogeny sent from Gregory to Hrdlicka, Hrdlicka Collection.

59. Keith 1931, p. 22. While writing this book, Keith reviewed Dart's monograph on the Taung fossil. It is difficult to say whether or not Keith realized that his extensive treatment of *Australopithecus* would become one of the reasons why Dart's detailed description was rejected by the Royal Society.

60. Ibid., pp. 115–116.

61. Zuckerman 1933, p. 6.

62. Ibid., p. 170.

63. Ibid., p. 172.

64. Ibid., pp. 176–177.

65. Hopwood 1933, p. 462.

66. Ibid., p. 460.

67. It is often suggested that Dubois became bitter after receiving a less

than enthusiastic reaction to his interpretation of *Pithecanthropus* as a missing link, and placed himself and his fossils in self-imposed isolation. Walker and Shipman (1996), however, suggested that he simply moved on without any clear vendetta against the scientific community that thwarted him. This latter opinion is difficult to support, since Dubois later maintained a different, but equally unorthodox opinion of his original find. He eventually claimed that the Trinil skull was in fact that of an ape, and was completely different from the *Sinanthropus* material and unlike the second adult *Pithecanthropus* skull discovered at Sangiran by von Koenigswald in 1937.

68. Formerly known as Choukoudian.

69. In the *Proceedings of the Zoological Society of London for 1931* (vol. 1, p. 348) there is unfortunately only a brief mention of the two presentations.

70. Linton 1936, pp. 14–15.

71. McGregor 1938, pp. 29–30.

72. Although there were a few voices who still objected to an ape ancestry for humans, one of the main critics, H. F. Osborn, died in 1935. Two authorities who were more supportive of Dart, geologist William Sollas and neuroanatomist Grafton Elliot Smith, died in 1936 and 1937, respectively.

73. See Findlay 1972 for a full biography on Broom.

74. Broom 1950a, p. 39.

75. These sites included Schurweberg and Gladysvale; years later australopithecine teeth were found at the latter site.

76. Another of Dart's students, Trevor Jones, had recovered some fossils from Sterkfontein in 1935, and published a paper on the fossil baboons he collected there (Jones 1936). The fact that several of Dart's students knew about the fossils at Sterkfontein, and probably told him of the site, suggests that Dart did not have the time or the inclination to search for further evidence of *Australopithecus*. Although Schepers went on to collaborate with Broom on the first full-length monograph about the South African fossils in 1945–46, he resented that "Broom had seized the opportunity to take over their site" (Findlay 1972, p. 66).

77. Broom 1950a, p. 44. The exact date of discovery is equivocal; in Broom's first publication on the new find (Broom 1936a), it appears that the find was made in late July, not August as he stated in 1950.

78. Broom 1936a, p. 488.

79. Broom 1936b, p. 476.

80. Broom 1938b, p. 868.

81. Schwarz 1936, p. 969.

82. Broom 1938b, p. 310.

83. Broom 1938c, p. 377. It is noteworthy that based on the young male mandibular fragment Broom later stated, "The remarkably chimpanzee-like symphysis is interesting in view of the condition found in the Piltdown mandible. I must classify myself with those who consider that there is no reasonable

doubt that this is the mandible of the same individual as has supplied the skull. . . . It seems quite likely that this Australopith character was retained in Eoanthropus though lost in later man."

84. Broom 1939, p. 304. Broom gained a reputation as a taxonomic "splitter," since he routinely erected new names for the australopithecine finds, usually at the genus level. In an interview with author John Reader, Dart stated that he thought this tendency came from Broom's prior paleontological work on mammallike reptiles, in which generic distinctions based on fragmentary fossils were very common.

85. Letter from Broom to Gregory, 27 Sept. 1938, Gregory Collection #1, Box 3.

86. Broom 1938b, p. 310.

87. Broom 1938d, p. 897.

88. Ibid., p. 896.

89. Reference here is to the first adult "Java Man" specimen recovered since Dubois found the original in 1891 (the cranium of a juvenile was collected at Modjokerto the previous year). The partial cranium, *Pithecanthropus* II, was collected in 1937 (von Koenigswald 1937), and, along with the numerous similar specimens from China, demonstrated that primitive humans did occupy the Far East during the Pleistocene. Ironically, Dubois at this point was insisting that his original fossil belonged to a giant gibbon.

90. Anon. 1938, p. 908.

91. Shaw 1939, p. 117.

92. Broom and Schepers 1946, p. 63.

93. Gregory 1916, p. 256.

94. Gregory 1922, p. 387.

95. Letter from Broom to Gregory, Mar. 1938, quoted in Gregory and Hellman 1939b, p. 559.

96. Quoted in Findlay 1972, p. 71.

97. Letter from Gregory to Raikes, 28 Dec. 1938, Gregory Collection #1, Box 9 (contained in the Hellman correspondence folder).

98. On p. 370 of Gregory and Hellman 1939c, the authors officially designate the Australopithecinae as a new subfamily.

99. Gregory and Hellman 1939a, p. 616.

100. Gregory and Hellman 1939b, p. 560.

101. Gregory and Hellman 1939c, p. 352.

102. Ibid., p. 363.

103. Gregory and Hellman 1939b, p. 564.

104. Andrews 1945, p. 57.

105. Hooton 1946, p. 278.

106. Ibid., p. 288.

Chapter 5. Darwin Redux

1. Leakey 1974, p. 196.

2. See Tattersall and Schwartz 2000, and other recent writings by both authors arguing that the synthesis in some ways reinforced certain elements inherent in the (temporalized) Great Chain concept, most notably gradual, anagenetic evolutionary change as opposed to punctuated equilibrium/rapid speciation, and concomitant taxonomic conservatism ("lumping").

3. Dart 1940, p. 23.

4. Ibid., p. 24.

5. Senyurek 1941, p. 300.

6. Ibid., pp. 300–301.

7. Ibid., p. 300 (fn).

8. Howells was one of the earliest professionally trained physical anthropologists in the United States. Like almost all of the American physical anthropologists of his generation, he was trained by E. A. Hooton at Harvard University. Howells eventually returned to Harvard in 1954, and remained there until his retirement in 1974.

9. Howells 1944, p. 102.

10. Ibid., p. 125.

11. Ibid.

12. Broom and Schepers 1946, p. 5.

13. Ibid, p. 3.

14. Ibid., p. 142.

15. Ibid., p. 123.

16. This debate continues today; see, for example, Ward 2002.

17. Letter from Keith to Broom, 11 May 1944, quoted in Broom and Schepers 1946, pp. 22–23.

18. Keith 1947, p. 377.

19. Both of Le Gros Clark's grandfathers held positions at St. Thomas's, and his paternal grandfather, Frederick, later went on to become president of the Royal College of Surgeons. One of Le Gros Clark's instructors was Ruggles Gates.

20. A detailed account of Le Gros Clark's life can be found in his autobiography, *Chant of Pleasant Exploration,* Edinburgh: E.& S. Livingstone, 1968.

21. Clark 1939, p. 121.

22. Clark 1940, p. 203.

23. Ibid., p. 210.

24. Quoted in Findlay 1972, p. 77.

25. Ibid.

26. Ibid., p. 78.

27. Clark 1946a, p. 863.

28. Ibid., pp. 863–864.

29. Clark, 1946b, p. 82.

30. Clark 1967, pp. 31–32.

31. In many of his papers published subsequent to his visit to South Africa, Le Gros Clark made a point of saying that those interested in the fossils needed to see the originals, as much of the critical morphology was diminished in the available casts. For example: "It may be said, however, that these human characters obtrude themselves much more forcibly on the notice in an examination of the original material than in an examination of casts." Clark 1952, pp. 112–113.

32. Clark 1967, p. 32.

33. Letter from Le Gros Clark to family, 25 Dec. 1946, Le Gros Clark Collection, Bodleian Library, Oxford.

34. Letter from Le Gros Clark to family, 31 Dec. 1946, Le Gros Clark Collection.

35. Broom 1952, p. 110.

36. This may have been the "important announcement" that was promised in the local Kenyan newspaper, the *East African Standard,* on January 10. In a letter back home, Le Gros Clark claimed to have no idea what this announcement was supposed to be. It is possible that someone leaked his new conclusion to the press in order to bring some attention to the congress.

37. Clark 1952, p. 113.

38. Although Leakey classified the Olduvai fossil as an australopithecine, he gave it a different genus name, *Zinjanthropus,* since he believed that in its morphology and especially its ability to make tools to a "set and regular pattern" it was much more human than any of the South African species.

39. Clark 1947, p. 300.

40. Ibid., pp. 331–332.

41. Letter from Le Gros Clark to Keith, 9 Aug. 1947, Keith Collection, Box KL1, Envelope L, Royal College of Surgeons, London.

42. Broom and Robinson 1947b, p. 431.

43. Dart 1952, p. 103. This passage is all the more remarkable when one considers that it was written *before* any australopithecines had even been found!

44. Le Gros Clark pointed out this feature to Dart when he visited Johannesburg to study the Taung infant in 1946. In one of his own publications (Clark 1947b) Le Gros Clark not only discussed the rate of attrition of the milk teeth compared with the first molar in Taung, but also pointed out that in the adult specimens from Sterkfontein and Kromdraai there was significant differential wear from M1 to M2 to M3, which similarly suggested a slow maturation rate, as in humans.

45. Dart 1948b, pp. 144, 151.

46. Ibid.

47. Clark 1948b, pp. 178–179.

48. Clark 1949b, p. 258. This lecture, subsequently published in the Society's quarterly journal, is also important since it provided the first real quantitative

analysis of the australopithecine crania. Le Gros Clark would later get into an extended debate with his former colleague at Oxford Solly Zuckerman over the use (and misuse) of statistical data in the study of the South African forms. Zuckerman continued to challenge any hominid claims for the australopithecines even after most members of the scientific community had come around to agree with Le Gros Clark (e.g., compare Clark 1951 with Ashton and Zuckerman 1950).

49. Dart believed that many of the broken animal bones he had found in association with the *A. prometheus* fossils were intentionally fashioned tools, which he named the osteodontokeratic (bone, tooth, horn) culture.

50. Dart 1949b, p. 257.

51. A partial calotte collected at about the same time was thought to come from a large baboon, due to the presence of a small sagittal crest. After a fairly complete female *Paranthropus crassidens* cranium displaying a similar crest was later recovered, it was discovered that the "baboon" calotte actually conjoined with the female maxilla. It is also of some interest that the presence of the sagittal crest briefly reopened the possibility that *Paranthropus*, and by extension the other australopithecines, was related to the gorilla (see, for example, the exchange of letters in the December 1950 issue of the *South African Journal of Science*, pp. 142–143, between Broom and South African geologist Lester King).

52. Broom 1949b, p. 903.

53. Broom and Robinson 1949, p. 379. The authors suspected that Dart's new species was also on the threshold of humanity, if not human: "This being [from Makapansgat] was described by Professor Dart about two years ago and named by him *Australopithecus prometheus*. We differ from Dart in considering that this form should probably be placed in a different genus from the Taungs ape-man and we consider it a more human type" (Broom and Robinson 1950e, pp. 493–494). Also, "At Makapan we have a fifth type [of australopith] which Dart has called *Australopithecus prometheus;* but this seems to be so nearly on the borderline between ape-man and man that on the evidence we have we cannot be quite certain which to call it" (Broom and Robinson 1950c, p. 151).

54. Broom 1949c, p. xliii.

55. Broom and Robinson 1950a, p. 57.

56. Broom & Robinson 1950b, p. 844.

57. Broom & Robinson 1950d, pp. 298–300.

58. Warren 1951, p. 5.

59. Ibid.

60. Schultz 1951, p. 51.

61. Ibid.

62. Simpson 1951, p. 55.

63. Ibid., p. 57.

64. Simpson 1945, p. 188.

65. Simpson 1951, p. 58.

66. Washburn 1951a, p. 651.

67. Simpson 1951, p. 63.
68. Washburn 1950, p. 246.
69. Washburn 1951b, p. 67.
70. Ibid., p. 74.
71. Ibid., p. 75.
72. Ibid., pp. 75–76.
73. Washburn 1951c, p. 298.
74. Ibid., p. 299.
75. Ibid.
76. Howells 1951, p. 79.
77. Ibid., pp. 82–83.
78. Ibid., p. 84.
79. Clark 1949b, p. 227.
80. Howells 1951, p. 82.
81. Ibid., p. 81.
82. Ibid., p. 82.
83. Mayr 1951, p. 109.
84. Ibid., p. 115.
85. Ibid., p. 114.
86. The modern taxonomic methodology called cladistics insists that morphology in and of itself is completely secondary to phylogeny in classifying organisms. At least some modern scholars, however, maintain that classification should include some room for gradistic, or adaptive, distinction. In the case of the living hominoids, although it is now quite certain that the African apes are our closest living relatives they continue to be categorized as members of the Pongidae. Cladists have naturally abandoned this classification and have included the chimpanzee and the gorilla in the Hominidae, leaving the orangutan as the only extant member of the Pongidae. Others continue to adhere to the traditional classification, arguing that to place humans with the African apes to the exclusion of the orangutan ignores the highly derived nature of our species. For them, the similar adaptive niche occupied by all of the great apes, which is quite different from that occupied by at least the more recent members of the Hominidae, warrants taxonomic distinction for humans. It is not likely that this situation will ever be resolved to everyone's satisfaction.

Epilogue

1. See Tobias 1998 for a characteristically thorough discussion that summarizes early interpretations of the australopithecine fossils, but makes no mention of the theoretical changes that were occurring as additional remains were being discovered.

2. See Tattersall 2000 and Foley 2001 for a debate on how the synthesis has specifically affected the field of paleoanthropology.

3. Original Piltdown protagonist Sir Arthur Smith Woodward passed away in 1944. Of the four initial respondents to Dart's 1925 paper, Woodward was by far the most critical.

4. Boule and Vallois 1957, pp. 91–92. This quote is from the 1957 English translation of the fourth edition.

5. Quoted in Morell 1995, pp. 188–189.

6. Leakey 1953, p. 182.

7. Ibid.

8. von Koenigswald 1954, pp. 796–797.

9. von Koenigswald 1956, p. 164.

10. Just about the time that these first absolute dates were being reported, slightly older and more humanlike hominids were being discovered at Olduvai. In 1964 these fossils were described as the "real" toolmakers and christened *Homo habilis*.

11. *Ramapithecus* was still considered to be a stem hominid throughout the 1970s, but was later shown to be a small species within a complex lineage whose only living representative is the orangutan. The phylogenetic position of *Kenyapithecus* remains unclear (Ward et al. 1999), although it is no longer considered to be a direct human ancestor.

12. Oddly, despite collecting a partial skeleton at Hadar (AL-288 ["Lucy"]) along with many other isolated elements, Johanson et al. chose a partial mandible from Laetoli (LH4) as the type specimen.

13. See White 2003 for an example of how the diversity of the early hominid record may be illusory, at least in the particular case of the middle Pliocene genus *Kenyanthropus* (Leakey et al. 2001). A particular scientist's interpretation of the diversity found in the fossil record is influenced by his or her view of how evolution works. Those who subscribe to a traditional gradualist, neo-Darwinian view tend to view diversity as intraspecific, or at least as representing different temporal points in a single evolving lineage (anagenesis). Those who have internalized a punctuated equilibrium model see many more branching events in evolving lineages, and interpret diversity as evidence of distinct speciation events in which new taxa are created.

14. On the other hand, it is possible that the simple act of becoming upright might have initially produced few significant changes in ecology and behavior. It is very tempting to imagine that the "event" in which the earliest hominids veered onto a separate evolutionary path from that leading to the living African apes was one of great import. After all, had this not taken place *Homo sapiens* would not be around to write about its prehistory. Yet there are no known cultural remains associated with the earliest hominids, and reconstruction of their habitats suggests that they were living in or near forests. It is becoming increasingly evident that the early evolution of our biological family did not involve any radical changes in lifestyle, and that the most important

advantages resulting from habitual bipedalism (e.g., thermoregulation and manipulative abilities) probably appeared much later.

15. Berger's analysis (a collaboration with Henry McHenry of the University of California at Davis) was largely based on a fragmentary skeleton from Sterkfontein, StW431. Presently, Ron Clarke of the University of the Witwatersrand is excavating what appears to be a nearly complete skeleton, StW573, also from Sterkfontein, which will allow the testing of the theory that South African and eastern African early hominids had different limb proportions (Clarke 1998).

16. The discoverers of the Chad mandible, while initially describing the specimen as "most similar in morphology to *Australopithecus afarensis*," ultimately decided to erect a new species, *Australopithecus bahrelghazali*.

17. Future discovery of fossils attributable to the extant African ape lineage(s) may also modify this definition.

Bibliography

Abel, W. 1931. Kritische Untersuchungen uber *Australopithecus africanus. Gegenbauer's Morphologische Jahrbuch* 65:539–640.

Aldrovandi, U. 1637. *De quadrupedibus digitatus viviparis*, Bolognai Berni.

Andrews, R. C. 1945. *Meet Your Ancestors*. New York: Viking.

Anon. 1925. The Taungs skull. *Brit. Med. J.* 28, March:622.

Anon. 1938. Anthropoid evolution in South Africa. *Nature* 142:908.

Aristotle. 1965 (Fourth century B.C.). *Historia Animalia*. English translation by A. L. Peck. Cambridge: Harvard University Press.

Ashton, E. H., and Zuckerman, S. 1950. Some quantitative dental characters of fossil anthropoids. *Phil. Trans. Roy. Soc. B* 234 (617):485–520.

Battell, A. 1967 (1624). The strange adventures of Andrew Battell. In *Purchas His Pilgrimes*, E. G. Ravenstein, ed. Nedeln, Liechtenstein: Kraus Reprint (reprinted from 1901 Hakluyt Society edition).

Bendysche, T. 1864. The history of anthropology. *Memoirs, Anthro. Soc. London* 1:335–458.

Berger, L. R. 2002. Early hominid body proportions and emerging complexities in human evolution. *Evol. Anth.* 11 (Supplement 1):42–44.

Blumenschine, R. J., et al. 2003. Late Pliocene *Homo* and hominid land use from Western Olduvai Gorge, Tanzania. *Science* 299:1217–1221.

Boule, M., and Vallois, H. 1957. *Fossil Men*. English translation of the 4th edition (1952), with some revisions, by M. Bullock. New York: Dryden.

Bowler, P. J. 1986. *Theories of Human Evolution: A Century of Debate, 1844–1944*. Baltimore: Johns Hopkins University Press.

Bowler, P. J. 1989. *Evolution: The History of an Idea*, 2nd ed. Berkeley: University of California Press.

Broom, R. 1918. The evidence afforded by the Boskop skull of a new species of primitive man, *Homo capensis*. *Anthro. Pap. Amer. Mus. Nat. Hist.* 23 (2):63–79.

Broom, R. 1925a. Some notes on the Taung skull. *Nature* 115:569–571.

Broom, R. 1925b. On the newly discovered South African man-ape. *Nat. Hist.* 25 (4):409–418.

Broom, R. 1925c. The Boskop skull. *Nature* 116:897.

Broom, R. 1926. The Boskop skull. *Nature* 117:589.

Broom, R. 1929. Note on the milk dentition of *Australopithecus*. *Proc. Zool. Soc. Lond.* 1929 (1):85–88.

Broom, R. 1930a. The age of *Australopithecus*. *Nature* 125:814.

Broom, R. 1930b. *The Origin of the Human Skeleton*. London: Witherby.

Broom, R. 1934. On the fossil remains associated with *Australopithecus africanus*. *S. Afr. J. Sci.* 31:471–480.

Broom, R. 1936a. A new fossil anthropoid skull from South Africa. *Nature* 138:486–488.

Broom, R. 1936b. A new ancestral link between ape and man. *Illust. Lond. News* Sept. 19, 1936:476–477.

Broom, R. 1936c. The dentition of *Australopithecus*. *Nature* 138:719.

Broom, R. 1938a. A step nearer to the missing link? A fossil ape with "human" teeth. *Illustr. Lond. News* May 14, 1938:868.

Broom, R. 1938b. The missing link no longer missing? *Illustr. Lond. News* Aug. 20, 1938:310–311.

Broom, R. 1938c. The Pleistocene anthropoid apes of South Africa. *Nature* 142:377–379.

Broom, R. 1938d. Further evidence on the structure of the South African Pleistocene anthropoids. *Nature* 142:897–899.

Broom, R. 1939. The dentition of the Transvaal Pleistocene anthropoids, *Plesianthropus* and *Paranthropus*. *Ann. Trans. Mus.* 19 (3):303–314.

Broom, R. 1947. Discovery of a new skull of the South African ape-man, *Plesianthropus*. *Nature* 159:672.

Broom, R. 1949a. Another new type of fossil ape-man. *Nature* 163:57.

Broom, R. 1949b. Jaw of the ape-man *Paranthropus crassidens. Nature* 163:903.

Broom, R. 1949c. The South African ape-men, and the age of the deposits in which they occur. *Quart. J. Geol. Soc. (Proceedings).* 105 (2):xlii–xliii.

Broom, R. 1950a. *Finding the Missing Link*. London: Watts and Co.

Broom, R. 1950b. The genera and species of the South African fossil apemen. *Amer. J. Phys. Anthro.* 8 (1):1–13.

Broom, R. 1952. The fossil ape-men of South Africa. In *Proceedings of the Pan-African Congress on Prehistory, 1947*, L. S. B. Leakey, ed. (asst. Sonia Cole). New York: Philosophical Library, pp. 107–111.

Broom, R., and Robinson, J. T. 1947a. Jaw of the male Sterkfontein apeman. *Nature* 160:153.

Broom, R., and Robinson, J. T. 1947b. Further remains of the Sterkfontein ape-man, *Plesianthropus. Nature* 160:430–431.

Broom, R., and Robinson, J. T. 1949. Man and ape-man: New discoveries from South Africa which supply two links of the evolutionary chain between the apes and man. *Illustr. Lond. News* Sept. 10, 1949: 378–379.

Broom, R., and Robinson, J. T. 1950a. One of the earliest types of man. *South Afr. J. Sci.* 47:55–57.

Broom, R., and Robinson, J. T. 1950b. Ape or man? *Nature* 166:843–844.

Broom, R., and Robinson, J. T. 1950c. Man contemporaneous with the Swartkrans ape-man. *Amer. J. Phys. Anthro.* 8:151–155.

Broom, R., and Robinson, J. T. 1950d. Note on the skull of the Swartkrans ape-man, *Paranthropus crassidens*. *Amer. J. Phys. Anthro.* 8:295–303.

Broom, R., and Robinson, J. T. 1950e. Notes on the pelves of the fossil ape-men. *Amer. J. Phys. Anthro.* 8:489–494.

Broom, R., and Robinson, J. T. 1952. *The Swartkrans ape-man, Paranthropus crassidens*. Pretoria: Transvaal Museum Memoir No. 6.

Broom, R., Robinson, J. T., and Schepers, G. W. H. 1950. *Sterkfontein ape-man Plesianthropus.* Pretoria: Transvaal Museum Memoir No. 4.

Broom, R., and Schepers, G. W. H. 1946. *The South African Fossil Ape-Men the Australopithecinae*. Pretoria: Transvaal Museum Memoir No. 2.

Brunet, M., et al. 1995. The first australopithecine 2,500 kilometres west of the Rift Valley (Chad). *Nature* 378:273–275.

Brunet, M., et al. 1996. *Australopithecus bahrelghazali,* une nouvelle espece d'Hominide ancien de al region de Koro Toro (Tchad). *C. R. Acad. Sci.* 322 (10):907–913.

Brunet, M., et al. 2002. A new hominid from the Upper Miocene of Chad, Central Africa. *Nature* 418:145–151.

Buffon, G. 1766. *Natural History, Volume 10: The Nomenclature of Apes.* Paris: L'Imprimerie Royale.

Burkhardt, R. W., Jr. 1995. *The Spirit of System: Lamarck and Evolutionary Biology.* Cambridge: Harvard University Press.

Camper, P. 1779. Account of the Organs of Speech of the Orang Outang. *Phil. Trans. Roy. Soc. Lond.* 69(1):139–159.

Cartmill, M. 1990. Human uniqueness and theoretical content in paleoanthropology. *Int. J. Primat.* 11:173–192.

Cartmill, M. 2001. Taxonomic revolutions and the animal-human boundary. In *Studying Human Origins: Disciplinary History and Epistemology*, R. Corbey and W. Roebroeks, eds. Amsterdam: Amsterdam University Press, pp. 97–106.

Cave, A. J. E. 1941. The Sterkfontein tooth. *Brit. Dent. J.* 70: 222–223.

Chazen, M. 1995. The meaning of *Homo sapiens*. In *Ape, Man, Apeman: Changing Views since 1600,* R. Corbey and B. Theunissen, eds. Leiden: Leiden University Dept. of Prehistory, pp. 229–240.

Clark, W. E. Le Gros. 1934. *Early Forerunners of Man*. London: Bailliere, Tindall, and Cox.

Clark, W. E. Le Gros. 1939. The interpretation of human fossils. *Modern Quarterly* 2:115–127.

Clark, W. E. Le Gros. 1940. Palaeontological evidence bearing on human evolution. *Biological Reviews* 15:202–230.

Clark, W. E. Le Gros. 1946a. Significance of the Australopithecinæ. *Nature* 157:863–865.

Clark, W. E. Le Gros. 1946b. Immediate problems of human palæontology. *Man* 72:80–84.

Clark, W. E. Le Gros. 1947a. Observations on the anatomy of the fossil Australopithecinæ. *J. Anatomy* 81:300.

Clark, W. E. Le Gros. 1947b. The importance of the fossil Australopithecinæ in the study of human evolution. *Science Progress* 35(139):377–395.

Clark, W. E. Le Gros. 1948a. African fossil primates discovered during 1947. *Nature* 161:667–669.

Clark, W. E. Le Gros. 1948b. Observations on certain rates of somatic evolution in the primates. In *Special Publication of the Royal Society of South Africa. Robert Broom Commemorative Volume*, A. L. DuToit, ed. Capetown: Royal Society of South Africa, pp. 171–180.

Clark, W. E. Le Gros. 1949a. *History of the Primates: An Introduction to the Study of Fossil Man*. London: British Museum of Natural History.

Clark, W. E. Le Gros. 1949b. New Palaeontological evidence bearing on the evolution of the Hominoidea. *Quart. J. Geol. Soc.* 105(2):225–264.

Clark, W. E. Le Gros. 1951. Comments on the dentition of the fossil Australopithecinae. *Man* 37:18–20.

Clark, W. E. Le Gros. 1952. Anatomical studies of fossil Hominoidea from Africa. In *Proceedings of the Pan-African Congress on Prehistory, 1947*, L. S. B. Leakey, ed. (asst. Sonia Cole). New York: Philosophical Library, pp. 111–115.

Clark, W. E. Le Gros. 1955. *The Fossil Evidence for Human Evolution*. Chicago: Chicago University Press.

Clark, W. E. Le Gros. 1960. *The Antecendents of Man*. Chicago: Chicago University Press.

Clark, W. E. Le Gros. 1967. *Man-Apes or Ape-Men?* New York: Holt, Rinehart and Winston.

Clarke, R. J. 1998. First ever discovery of a well-preserved skull and associated skeleton of *Australopithecus*. *S. Afr. J. Sci.* 94:460–463.

Collard, M., and Wood, B. 2000. How reliable are human phylogenetic hypotheses? *Proc. Nat. Acad. Sci.* 97(9), 5003–5006.

Coppens, Y., Howell, F. C., Isaac, G. L., and Leakey, R. E. F., eds. 1976. *Earliest Man and Environments in the Lake Rudolf Basin*. Chicago: University of Chicago Press.

Cunningham, D. J. 1895a. Dr. Dubois' so-called missing-link? *Nature* 51:428–429.

Cunningham, D. J. 1895b. Dr. Dubois' "missing link." *Nature* 53:115–116.

Cunningham, D. J. 1896. The place of "Pithecanthropus" on the genealogical tree. *Nature* 53:296.

Cunningham, D. J. 1908. Anthropology in the eighteenth century. *J. Roy. Anthro. Inst.* 38:10–35.

Dart, R. A. 1925a. *Australopithecus africanus:* The man-ape of South Africa. *Nature* 115:195–199.

Dart, R. A. 1925b. Africa, the cradle of humanity. *Illustr. Lond. News* June 13, 1925:1154–1155.

Dart, R. A. 1925c. A note on Makapansgat: A site of early human occupation. *S. Afr. J. Sci.* 22:454.

Dart, R. A. 1934. The dentition of Australopithecus africanus. *Folia Anatomica Japonica* 12:207–221.

Dart, R. A. 1940. Recent discoveries bearing on human history in southern Africa. *J. Roy. Anthro. Inst.* 70(1):13–27.

Dart, R. A. 1948a. The Makapansgat proto-human *Australopithecus prometheus. Amer. J. Phys. Anthro.* 6(3):259–283.

Dart, R. A. 1948b. The Infancy of Australopithecus. In *Special Publication of the Royal Society of South Africa, Robert Broom Commemorative Volume,* A. L. DuToit, ed. Capetown: Royal Society of South Africa.

Dart, R. A. 1948c. The adolescent mandible of *Australopithecus prometheus. Amer. J. Phys. Anthro.* 6(4):391–409.

Dart, R. A. 1949a. The cranio-facial fragment of *Australopithecus prometheus. Amer. J. Phys. Anthro.* 7(2):187–213.

Dart, R. A. 1949b. The first pelvic bones of *Australopithecus prometheus:* Preliminary note. *Amer. J. Phys. Anthro.* 7(2):255–257.

Dart, R. A. 1952. Faunal and climatic fluctuations in Makapaansgat [*sic*] valley: The irrelation to the geological age and Promethean status of Australopithecus. In *Proceedings of the Pan-African Congress on Prehistory, 1947,* L. S. B. Leakey, ed. (asst. Sonia Cole). New York: Philosophical Library, pp. 96–106.

Dart, R. A., and Craig, D. 1959. *Adventures with the Missing Link.* London: Hamish Hamilton.

Darwin, C. 1859. *The Origin of Species by Means of Natural Selection.* New York: Modern Library.

Darwin, C. 1871. *The Descent of Man and Selection in Relation to Sex.* New York: Modern Library.

Darwin, E. 1794. *Zoonomia, or The Laws of Organic Life,* volume 1. Dublin: P. Byrne and W. Jones.

Dawson, C., and Woodward, A. S. 1913. On the discovery of a Palaeolithic human skull and mandible in a flint-bearing gravel overlying the Wealden. *Quart. J. Geol. Soc.* 69:117–144.

Dubois, E. 1896. The place of "*Pithecanthropus*" in the genealogical tree. *Nature* 53:245–247.

Dubois, E. 1898. Pithecanthropus erectus: A form from the ancestral stock of mankind. *Ann. Rpt. Smith. Inst.* 1898:445–459.

Eiseley, L. C. 1946. Review of *The South African fossil ape men: The Australopithecinae,* by R. Broom and G. W. H. Schepers. *Science* 104:90.

Eiseley, L. 1954. The reception of the first missing links. *Proc. Amer. Phil. Soc.* 98(6):453–465.

Findlay, G. 1972. *Dr. Robert Broom, F.R.S.* Cape Town: Balkema.

Foley, R. 2001. In the shadow of the Modern Synthesis? Alternative perspectives on the last fifty years of paleoanthropology. *Evol. Anth.* 10(1):5–14.

Foucault, M. 1970 (1966). *The Order of Things.* English translation of the French *Les Mots et Les Choses.* New York: Pantheon.

Galen, C. 1956 (c. 192 A.D.). *On Anatomical Procedures.* English translation by C. Singer. Oxford: Oxford University Press.

Galen, C. 1962 (c. 192 A.D.). *On Anatomical Procedures: The Later Books.* English translation by W. L. H. Duckworth. Cambridge: Cambridge University Press.

Garner, R. L. 1900. *Apes and Monkeys.* Boston: Ginn and Co.

Gesner, K. 1551. *Historiae animalium. Vol. 1: De Quadrupedibus viviparis.* Tiguri. 1602 edition (Francofurti).

Goodman, M. 1963. Man's place in the phylogeny of the primates as reflected in serum proteins. In *Classification and Human Evolution,* S. L. Washburn, ed. Chicago: Aldine, pp. 204–234.

Gould, S. J. 1983. Chimp on the chain. *Natural History* Dec. 1983:18.

Grayson, D. K. 1983. *The Establishment of Human Antiquity.* New York: Academic.

Greene, J. C. 1959. *The Death of Adam: Evolution and Its Impact on Western Thought.* Ames: Iowa State University Press.

Gregory, W. K. 1914. The dawn man of Piltdown, England. *Amer. Mus. J.* 14:189–200.

Gregory, W. K. 1915. Is *Sivapithecus* Pilgrim an ancestor of man? *Science* 42:341–2.

Gregory, W. K. 1916. Studies on the evolution of the primates. *Bull. Amer. Mus. Nat. Hist.* 35:239–355.

Gregory, W. K. 1922. *The Origin and Evolution of the Human Dentition.* Baltimore: Williams and Wilkins.

Gregory, W. K. 1927. How near is the relationship of man to the chimpanzee-gorilla stock? *Quart. Rev. Bio.* 2:549–560.

Gregory, W. K. 1930a. A critique of Professor Osborn's theory of human origin. *Amer. J. Phys. Anth.* 14(2):133–161.

Gregory, W. K. 1930b. The origin of man from a brachiating anthropoid stock. *Science* 71: 645–650.

Gregory, W. K. 1946. Review of *The South African fossil ape men: The Australopithecinae,* by R. Broom and G. W. H. Schepers. *Amer. Nat.* 80:645–649.

Gregory, W. K., and Hellman, M. 1926. The dentition of *Dryopithecus* and the origin of man. *Anthro. Papers, Amer. Mus. Nat. Hist.* 28(1):1–124.

Gregory, W. K., and Hellman, M. 1938. Evidence of the australopithecine man-apes on the origin of man. *Science* 88:615–616.

Gregory, W. K., and Hellman, M. 1939a. Fossil man-apes of South Africa. *Nature* 143:25–26.

Gregory, W. K., and Hellman, M. 1939b. The South African fossil man-apes and the origin of the human dentition. *J. Amer. Dental Assoc.* 26:558–564.

Gregory, W. K., and Hellman, M. 1939c. The dentition of the extinct South African man-ape *Australopithecus* (*Plesianthropus transvaalensis* Broom: A comparative and phylogenetic study). *Annals. Trans. Mus.* 19(4):339–373.

Grine, F. 1993. Australopithecine taxonomy and phylogeny: Historical background and recent interpretation. In *The Human Evolution Source Book,* R. L. Ciochon and J. G. Fleagle, eds., Englewood Cliffs, N.J.: Prentice Hall, pp. 198–210.

Gruber, J. W. 1948. The Neanderthal controversy: Nineteenth-century version. *Scientific Monthly* 67:436–439.

Gundling, T. 1999. *All in the Family: A Revision of the Hominidae Be-*

tween 1925–1951. Ph.D. dissertation, Department of Anthropology, Yale University.

Gundling, T. 2002. Stand and be counted: A history of bipedalism as a marker of the human lineage. *Amer. J. Phys. Anth.* Supplement 34 (abstract): 79.

Gundling, T. 2003. Teleology and human phylogeny. *Amer. J. Phys. Anth.* Supplement 36 (abstract): 105–106.

Haile-Selassie, Y. 2001. Late Miocene hominids from the Middle Awash, Ethiopia. *Nature* 412:178–181.

Hartmann, R. 1886. *Anthropoid Apes.* New York: D. Appleton and Co.

Herodotus. 1996 (c. 440 B.C.). *Histories.* Hertfordshire: Wordsworth Editions.

Hooton, E. A. 1927. Where did man originate? *Antiquity* 1:133–150.

Hooton, E. A. 1931. *Up from the Ape.* New York: Macmillan.

Hooton, E. A. 1946. *Up from the Ape,* Revised. New York: Macmillan.

Hopwood, A. T. 1933. Miocene primates from Kenya. *J. Linn. Soc. (Zool.)* 38:437–464.

Howells, W. W. 1944. *Mankind So Far.* New York: Doubleday, Doran, and Co.

Howells, W. W. 1951. Origin of the human stock: Concluding remarks of the chairman. In *Origin and Evolution of Man,* vol. 15 of *Cold Spring Harbor Symposia on Quantitative Biology,* K. B. Warren, ed. pp. 79–86.

Howells, W. W. 1985. Taung: A mirror for American anthropology. In *Hominid Evolution: Past, Present and Future,* P. V. Tobias, ed. New York: Alan R. Liss, pp. 19–24.

Hrdlicka, A. 1916. *The Most Ancient Skeletal Remains of Man,* 2nd ed. Washington, D.C.: Smithsonian Institution.

Hrdlicka, A. 1925. The Taungs skull. *Amer. J. Phys. Anth.* 8(4): 379–392.

Hrdlicka, A. 1930. *Skeletal Remains of Early Man, Smithsonian Miscellaneous Collections* 83:1–379 (whole volume).

Hutton, J. 1794. *Theory of the Earth, with Proofs and Illustrations,* 2 vols. Edinburgh.

Huxley, J. 1942. *Evolution: The Modern Synthesis.* London: Allen and Unwin.

Huxley, T. H. 1890 (1863). On the relations of man to the lower animals. Reprinted in *Man's Place in Nature: Essays.* New York: D. Appleton and Co.

Huxley, T. H. 1864. Further remarks upon the human remains from the Neanderthal. *Nat. Hist. Rev.* 4:429–446.

Jaffe, M. 2000. *The Gilded Dinosaur*. New York: Crown.

Janson, W. H. 1952. *Apes and Ape Lore in the Middle Ages and the Renaissance*. London: Warburg Institute.

Johanson, D. C., and White, T. D. 1979. A systematic assessment of early African hominids. *Science* 202:321–330.

Johanson, D. C., White, T. D., and Coppens, Y. 1978. A new species of the genus *Australopithecus* (Primates: Hominidae) from the Pliocene of eastern Africa. *Kirtlandia* 28:1–14.

Jones, T. R. 1936. A new fossil primate from Sterkfontein, Krugersdorp, Transvaal. *S. Afr. J. Sci.* 33:709–728.

Keith, A. 1925a. *The Antiquity of Man,* 2nd ed. (2 vol.). Philadelphia: J.B. Lippincott.

Keith, A. 1925b. The fossil anthropoid ape from Taungs. *Nature* 115: 234–236.

Keith, A. 1925c. The new missing link. *Brit. Med. J.*, 14 Feb 1925:325–326.

Keith, A. 1925d. The Taungs skull. *Nature* 116:11.

Keith, A. 1931. *New Discoveries Relating to the Antiquity of Man*. London: Williams and Norgate.

Keith, A. 1947. Australopithecinae or Dartians? *Nature* 159:377.

Kennedy, K. A. R., and Ciochon, R. L. 1999. A canine tooth from the Siwaliks: First recorded discovery of a fossil ape? *Hum. Evol.* 14(3): 231–253.

Koenigswald, G. H. R. von. 1937. Pithecanthropus received into the human family tree. *Illustr. Lond. News* Dec. 11, 1937:1039–1041.

Koenigswald, G. H. R. von. 1956. *Meeting Prehistoric Man.* New York: Harper and Brothers.

Kohler, M., and Moya-Sola, S. 1997. Ape-like or hominid-like: The post-cranial behavior of *Oreopithecus bambolii* reconsidered. *PNAS* 94: 11747–11750.

Kuhn, T. 1970. *The Structure of Scientific Revolutions,* 2nd ed. Chicago: University of Chicago Press.

Kuntz, M. L. and P. G., eds. 1987. *Jacob's Ladder and the Tree of Life: Concepts of Hierarchy and the Great Chain of Being*. New York: Peter Lang.

Lamarck, J. B. 1963 (1809). *Zoological Philosophy*. English translation by H. Elliot. New York: Hafner.

Landau, M. 1991. *Narratives of Human Evolution*. New Haven: Yale University Press.

Lartet, E. 1837. Rapport sur la decouverte de plusieurs ossements fossiles de quadrumanes, dans le depot tertiaire de Sansan. *Compte Rendus L'Acad. Sci.* 4(26):981–998.

Lartet, E. 1856. Note sur un grand Singe fossile qui se rattache au groupe des Singes superieurs. *Compte Rendus L'Acad. Sci.* 43:219–223.

Leakey, L. S. B. 1953. *Adam's Ancestors,* 4th ed. London: Methuen.

Leakey, L. S. B. 1959. A new fossil skull from Olduvai. *Nature* 184:491–493.

Leakey, L. S. B. 1962. A new lower Pliocene fossil primate from Kenya. *The Annals and Magazine of Nat. Hist.* 13(4), #47: 689–694.

Leakey, L. S. B. 1974. *By the Evidence: Memoirs, 1932–1951*. New York: Harcourt, Brace, Jovanovich.

Leakey, L. S. B., and Cole, S. 1952. *Proceedings of the Pan-African Congress on Prehistory, 1947*. New York: Philosophical Library.

Leakey, L. S. B., Evernden, J. F., and Curtis, G. H. 1961. Age of Bed I, Olduvai Gorge, Tanganyika. *Nature* 191:478–479.

Leakey, M. G., Feibel, C. S., McDougall, I., and Walker, A. 1994. New four-million-year-old hominid species from Kanapoi and Allia Bay, Kenya. *Nature* 376:565–571.

Leakey, M. G., et al. 2001. New hominin genus from eastern Africa shows diverse middle Pliocene lineages. *Nature* 410:433–440.

Lewin, R. 1987. *Bones of Contention: Controversies in the Search for Human Origins*. New York: Touchstone.

Lieberman, D. E. 2001. Another face in our family tree. *Nature* 410:419–420.

Linnaeus, C. 1939 (1758). *Systema Naturae,* 10th ed. photographic facsimile. London: British Museum of Natural History.

Linton, R. 1936. *The Study of Man*. New York: Appleton-Century-Crofts.

Lovejoy, A. O. 1936. *The Great Chain of Being*. Cambridge: Harvard University Press.

Lubbock, J. 1865. *Prehistoric Times*. London: Williams and Norgate.

Lydekker, R. 1879. Further notes of Siwalik mammalia. *Rec. Geol. Surv. India* 12(1):33–52.

Lydekker, R. 1896. Siwalik mammalia—Supplement 1. *Palaeont. Mem. Geol. Surv. India* ser. 10, vol. 4(1):1–18.

Lydekker, R. 1915. Recent work on vertebrate palaeontology. *Nature* 95:276–277.

Mayr, E. 1951. Taxonomic categories in fossil hominids. In *Origin and Evolution of Man*, vol. 15 of *Cold Spring Harbor Symposia on Quantitative Biology*, K. B. Warren, ed. pp. 109–118.

Mayr, E., and Provine, W. B., eds. 1980. *The Evolutionary Synthesis: Perspectives on the Unification of Biology*. Cambridge: Harvard University Press.

McCabe, J. 1910. *Prehistoric Man*. London: Milner and Co.

McDermott, W. C. 1938. *The Ape in Antiquity*. Baltimore: Johns Hopkins University Press.

McGregor, J. H. 1938. Human origins and early man. In *General Anthropology*, F. Boas, ed. Boston: D. C. Heath and Co., pp. 24–94.

Miller, G. S. 1928. The controversy over human "missing links." *Ann. Rpt. Smith. Inst.* 1928.

Mivart, St. G. 1874. *Man and Apes*. New York: D. Appleton and Co.

Montagu, M. F. A. 1943. Edward Tyson, M.D., F.R.S. 1650–1708 and the rise of human and comparative anatomy in England. *Memoirs Amer. Phil. Soc.* 20:225–419.

Moore, R. 1953. *Man, Time and Fossils: The Story of Evolution*. New York: Alfred A. Knopf.

Morell, V. 1995. *Ancestral Passions: The Leakey Family and the Quest for Humankind's Beginnings*. New York: Simon and Schuster.

Morse, E. S. 1884. Man in the Tertiaries. *Proc. Amer. Assoc. Adv. Sci.* 33: 3–15.

Nuttall, G. H. F. 1904. *Blood Immunity and Blood Relationship*. London: Cambridge University Press.

Osborn, H. F. 1927. *Man Rises to Parnassus*. Princeton, N.J.: Princeton University Press.

Osborn, H. F. 1930. The discovery of Tertiary man. *Science* 71:1–7.

Pilgrim, G. E. 1915. New Siwalik primates and their bearing on the question of the evolution of man and the Anthropoidea. *Rec. Geol. Surv. India* 45:1–75.

Pliny the Elder. 1991 (c. 77 A.D.). *Natural History: A Selection.* London: Penguin.

Rainger, R. 1989. What's the use: William King Gregory and the functional morphology of the fossil vertebrates. *J. Hist. Biol.* 22(1):103–139.

Reader, J. 1981. *Missing Links*. London: Book Club Associates.

Reed, C. A. 1983. A short history of the discovery and early study of the australopithecines: The first find to the death of Robert Broom (1924–1951). In *Hominid Origins: Inquiries Past and Present,* K. J. Reichs, ed. Washington, D.C.: University Press of America, pp. 1–77.

Richmond, B. G., Begun, D. R., and Strait, D. S. 2001. Origin of human bipedalism: The knuckle-walking hypothesis revisited. *Yrbk. Phys. Anth.* 44:70–105.

Robinson, J. T. 1954. The genera and species of the Australopithecinae. *Amer. J. Phys. Anthro.* 12:181–200.

Ruvolo, M. E. 1997. Molecular phylogeny of the hominoids: Inferences from multiple independent DNA sequence data sets. *Mol. Biol. Evol.* 14:248–265.

Sarich, V. M., and Wilson, A. C. 1967. Immunological time scale for hominid evolution. *Science* 158:1200–1203.

Schaaffhausen, D. 1861 (1858). On the crania of the most ancient races of man. *Nat. Hist. Rev.* 1:155–176. (English translation by G. Busk.)

Schmitz, R. W., et al. 2002. The Neandertal type site revisited: Interdisciplinary investigations of skeletal remains from the Neander Valley, Germany. *Proc. Nat. Acad. Sci.* 99(20):13342–13347.

Schultz, A. H. 1951. The specializations of man and his place among the catarrhine primates. In *Origin and Evolution of Man,* vol. 15 of *Cold Spring Harbor Symposia on Quantitative Biology*, K. B. Warren, ed., pp. 37–53.

Schwarz, E. 1936. The Sterkfontein ape. *Nature* 138:969.

Senut, B., et al. 2001. First hominid from the Miocene (Lukeino formation, Kenya). *C.R. Acad. Sci., Paris* 332:137–144.

Senyurek, M. S. 1941. The dentition of *Plesianthropus* and *Paranthropus. Ann. Trans. Mus.* 20(3):293–302.

Senyurek, M. S. 1947. Review of *The South African fossil ape men: The Australopithecinae,* by R. Broom and G. W. H. Schepers. *Amer. J. Phys. Anthro.* 5(3):375–377.

Shaw, J. C. M. 1939. Further remains of a Sterkfontein ape. *Nature* 143:117.

Shapiro, H. 1981. Earnest A. Hooton, 1887–1954, *in Memoriam cum amore. Amer. J. Phys. Anthro.* 56(4):431–434.

Shipman, P. 2001. *The Man Who Found the Missing Link.* New York: Simon and Schuster.

Simons, E. L. 1961. The phyletic position of *Ramapithecus. Postilla* (Yale Peabody Museum of Natural History) 57(30):1–9.

Simons, E. L., and Pilbeam. D. R. 1965. Preliminary revision of the Dryopithecinae (Pongidae, Anthropoidea). *Folia Primatologia* 3:81–152.

Simpson, G. G. 1945. The principles of classification and a classification of the mammals. *Bull. Amer. Mus. Nat. Hist.* 85:i–xvi, 1–350 (whole volume).

Simpson, G. G. 1951. Some principles of historical biology bearing on human origins. In *Origin and Evolution of Man,* vol. 15 of *Cold Spring Harbor Symposia on Quantitative Biology,* K. B. Warren, ed. pp. 55–66.

Smith, G. E. 1924. *Essays on the Evolution of Man.* Oxford: Oxford University Press.

Smith, G. E. 1925a. The fossil anthropoid ape from Taungs. *Nature* 115:234–236.

Smith, G. E. 1925b. Australopithecus, the man-like ape from Bechuanaland. *Illustr. Lond. News* Feb. 14, 1925:237–241.

Smith, G. E. 1925c. Exhibitions and notices. *Proc. Zool. Soc. Lond.* 1925(2):1238.

Sollas, W. J. 1925. The Taungs skull. *Nature* 115:908–909.

Spencer, F. 1981. The rise of academic physical anthropology in the United States (1880–1980): A historical overview. *Amer. J. Phys. Anthro.* 56(4):353–364.

Spencer, F. 1990. *Piltdown, A Scientific Forgery.* Oxford: Oxford University Press.

St. Augustine. 1984 (c. 427 A.D.). *City of God.* English translation by H. Bettenson. London: Penguin.

Stanford, C. 2001. *Significant Others: The Ape-Human Continuum and the Quest for Human Nature.* New York: Basic Books.

Stringer, C., and Gamble, C. 1993. *In Search of the Neanderthals.* New York: Thames and Hudson.

Tattersall, I. 1995. *The Fossil Trail: How We Know What We Think We Know About Human Evolution.* Oxford: Oxford University Press.

Tattersall, I. 2000. Paleoanthropology: The last half-century. *Evol. Anth.* 9(1):2–16.

Tattersall, I., and Schwartz, J. 2000. *Extinct Humans.* New York: Westview.

Thijssen, J. M. M. H. 1995. Reforging the great chain of being: The medieval discussion of the human status of "pygmies" and its influence on Edward Tyson. In *Ape, Man, Apeman: Changing Views since 1600,* R. Corbey and B. Theunissen, eds. Leiden: Leiden University Dept. of Prehistory, pp. 43–50.

Tobias, P. V. T. 1984. *Dart, Taung and the Missing Link.* Johannesburg: Witwatersrand University Press.

Tobias, P. V. T. 1997. Some little known chapters in the early history of the Makapansgat fossil hominid site. *Palaeont. Afr.* 33:67–79.

Tobias, P. V. T. 1998. Ape-like *Australopithecus* after seventy years: Was it a hominid? *J. Royal Anthrop. Inst.* 4(2): 283–308.

Trinkaus, E., and Shipman, P. 1992. *The Neandertals: Changing the Image of Mankind.* New York: Knopf.

Tulp, N. 1641. *Observationum medicarum libri tres.* Amsterdam.

Tyson, E. 1699. *Orang-Outang, sive Homo Sylvestris: or, the Anatomy of a Pygmie.* London: Dawson's of Pall Mall (1966).

Vogt, K. 1864. *Lectures on Man: His Place in Creation and in the History of the Earth.* London: Anthropological Society of London.

Walker, A., and Shipman, P. 1996. *The Wisdom of the Bones.* New York: Knopf.

Wallace, A. R. 1889. *Darwinism.* New York: Humboldt.

Ward, C. 2002. Interpreting the posture and locomotion of *Australopithecus afarensis:* Where do we stand? *Yrbk. Phys. Anth.* 45(supplement no. 35):185–215.

Ward, S., Brown, B., Hill, A., Kelley, J., and Downs, W. 1999. *Equatorius:* A new hominoid genus from the Middle Miocene of Kenya. *Science* 285:1382–1386.

Warren, K. B., ed. 1951. *Origin and Evolution of Man,* vol. 15 of *Cold Spring Harbor Symposia on Quantitative Biology*.

Washburn, S. L. 1950. Review of *Genetics, Palaeontology, and Evolution,* G. L. Jepsen, E. Mayr, and G. G. Simpson, eds. *Amer. J. Phys Anth.* 8:245–246.

Washburn, S. L. 1951a. Evolutionary importance of the South African "man-apes." *Nature* 167:650–651.

Washburn, S. L. 1951b. The analysis of primate evolution with particular reference to the origin of man. In *Origin and Evolution of* Man, vol. 15 of Cold *Spring Harbor Symposia on Quantitative Biology*, ed. K. B. Warren. pp. 67–78.

Washburn, S. L. 1951c. The new physical anthropology. *N.Y. Acad. Sci.* 13:298–304.

Wheelhouse, F. 1983. *Raymond Arthur Dart: A Pictorial Profile.* Sydney: Transpareon.

Wheelhouse, F., and Smithford, K. S. 2001. *Dart: Scientist and Man of Grit.* Sydney: Transpareon.

White, T. D. 2003. Early hominids—diversity or distortion? *Science* 299:1994–1997.

White, T. D., Suwa, G., and Asfaw, B. 1994. *Australopithecus ramidus,* a new species of early hominid from Aramis, Ethiopia. *Nature* 371:306–312.

White, T. D., Suwa, G., and Asfaw, B. 1995. Corrigendum. *Nature* 375:88.

Wilder, H. H. 1926. *Pedigree of the Human Race.* New York: Henry Holt and Co.

Wittkower, R. 1942. Marvels of the East: A study in the history of monsters. *J. Warburg and Courtauld Inst.* 5:159–197.

Wood, B. 2002. Hominid revelations from Chad. *Nature* 418:133–135.

Woodward, A. S. 1914. On the lower jaw of an anthropoid ape (*Dryopithecus)* from the upper Miocene of Lerida (Spain). *Quart. J. Geol. Soc.* 70:316–320.

Woodward, A. S. 1921. A new cave man from Rhodesia, South Africa. *Nature* 108:371–372.

Woodward, A. S. 1925. The fossil anthropoid ape from Taungs. *Nature* 115:234–236.

Yerkes, R. M. and A. W. 1929. *The Great Apes: A Study of Anthropoid Life.* New Haven: Yale University Press.

Zuckerman, S. 1933. *Functional Affinities of Man, Monkeys, and Apes.* New York: Harcourt, Brace and Co.

Index